MODERN GARDEN DESIGN
MODERNES GARTENDESIGN
JARDINS DESIGN & AMÉNAGEMENT
MODERN TUINIEREN
DISEÑO DE JARDINES

KÖNEMANN
is an imprint of
Frechmann Kolón GmbH
www.frechmann.com

© 2014 for this edition: Frechmann Kolón GmbH

Editorial project:
LOFT Publications
Barcelona, Spain
Tel.: +34 932 688 088
Fax: +34 932 687 073
loft@loftpublications.com
www.loftpublications.com

Editorial coordinator:
Simone K. Schleifer

Assistant to editorial coordination:
Aitana Lleonart Triquell

Editor:
Marta Serrats

Art director:
Mireia Casanovas Soley

Design and layout coordination:
Claudia Martínez Alonso

Layout:
Anabel N. Quintana

Translations:
Cillero & de Motta,
Equipo de Edición,
Mengès,
Antonio Moreno,
Kirstin Bleiel,
Volker Ellerbeck,
Catalina Rojas Hauser

Published in the United States in 2015 by:

Skyhorse Publishing
307 West 36th Street, 11th Floor
New York, NY 10018, USA
T: +1 212 643 6816
info@skyhorsepublishing.com
www.skyhorsepublishing.com

ISBN 978-3-86407-307-6 (GB)
ISBN 978-3-86407-305-2 (D)
ISBN 978-3-86407-308-3 (NL)
ISBN 978-3-86407-306-9 (E)
ISBN 978-1-63220-594-0 (Skyhorse, USA)

Printed in Spain

Gardens become an extension of our homes and encourage us to enjoy the outdoors. Whether it is a private garden or a park in a city, planning the elements that form part of this space is an absolute necessity. The list of plants, the strategic importance of its layout and the elements that will create an aesthetic dialogue (furniture, lighting and accessories) require good organization to fully enjoy life outdoors.

Maintaining green spaces that form part of the private and public sphere of our coexistence with vegetation, is essential to minimize the environmental impact. The implementation of green spaces creates a habitat for living organisms (plants, insects, birds, microscopic organisms), which in turn improves the microclimate of the surroundings due to the moisture contribution of the plant's, which absorb CO_2 and provide O_2. Also, from a personal point of view, a space with plants aesthetically improves the garden providing pure pleasure. It not only allows us to be in contact with nature and learn from it, but it gives us colors, aromas and sounds that stimulate our senses.

Currently, the upward trend of gardens and vegetable gardens contributes to the sustainability of our cities. Production that is as ecological as possible does not contaminate or degrade the environment. Creating an edible balcony, for example, is simple and very satisfying as it provides foods that have not been exposed to chemicals used in conventional agriculture. From vegetables and tubers to herbs, the result is always the result of the motivation, care and effort dedicated.

There also are several international initiatives to create viable ecological systems. The Green Guerrilla, for example, works to create communal gardens on abandoned rooftops or neglected lots of land, from the top of skyscrapers. The Earth Pledge Foundation has proposed to make the rooftops of New York green with a programme called Green Roofs as an attractive way to alleviate the pressure of the urban landscape.

This book presents a selection of green spaces that surround us, beginning with our homes extending to vegetated spaces that form part of our cities. Gardens, terraces, balconies, courtyards, parks, plazas, avenues, vegetated buildings are some of the examples that are presented in this book. It also offers advice to design the garden, opening the range to all possible outdoor locations.

Without a doubt, the examples included in this book are an invaluable guide to appreciate these beautiful green spaces that surround us. Learning to value our immediate environment is the best assurance for a sustainable future whether we live in the countryside or city.

Gärten werden zu Erweiterungen unserer Wohnungen und laden dazu ein, das Leben im Freien zu genießen. Unabhängig davon, ob es sich um einen heimischen Garten oder einen städtischen Park handelt, ist es notwendig, die einzelnen Elemente dieses Bereiches zu planen. Die Anordnung der verschiedenen Pflanzenarten und weiterer Elemente (Möblierung, Beleuchtung und Zubehör) ist von strategischer Bedeutung für einen ästhetischen Dialog und verlangt eine gute Organisation, damit man die Natur in vollen Zügen erleben kann.

Die Erhaltung der Grünzonen, die Teil unseres privaten und öffentlichen Lebensraums sind, ist unverzichtbar, um die Umweltbelastung zu reduzieren. Mit der Einführung von Grünzonen wird ein Lebensraum für lebendige Organismen (Pflanzen, Insekten, Vögel, Mikroorganismen) geschaffen, der seinerseits das Mikroklima der Umgebung verbessert, dank des Beitrags zur Feuchtigkeit der Pflanzen, die CO_2 absorbieren und O_2 liefern. Aber auch aus persönlicher Sicht verschönert die Vegetation den Garten und verschafft uns reine Freude. Der Garten ermöglicht es uns nicht nur, in Kontakt mit der Natur zu stehen und von ihr zu lernen, sondern er schenkt uns zudem Farben, Düfte und Töne, die unsere Sinne anregen.

Die Zunahme von Ziergärten und städtischer Obst- und Gemüsegärten trägt zur Nachhaltigkeit unserer Städte bei. Eine Produktion, die so ökologisch wie möglich ist, kontaminiert und zerstört die Umwelt nicht. Es ist z.B. einfach und sehr befriedigend, auf einem Balkon Nahrungsmittel zu ziehen, da man so Lebensmittel erhält, die nicht den Chemikalien, die in der konventionellen Landwirtschaft verwendet werden, ausgesetzt worden sind. Von Gemüse und Knollen bis zu Kräutern ist das Ergebnis immer die Frucht der Motivation, Sorgfalt und Mühe dessen, der sich ihnen widmet.

Es gibt aber auch zahlreiche internationale Initiativen für ökologische Systeme. So arbeitet z.B. die Green Guerilla für die Anlage von Gemeinschaftsgärten auf verlassenen Grundstücken oder ungenutzten Parzellen zwischen Hochhäusern. Und die Stiftung Earth Pledge hat es sich zur Aufgabe gemacht, die Dächer von New York mit einem *Grüne Dächer* genannten Programm zu begrünen: eine schöne Art, der Stadtlandschaft das Bedrückende zu nehmen.

Dieses Buch stellt eine Auswahl von grünen Bereichen vor, die uns umgeben, angefangen von unseren eigenen Wohnungen bis zu den Grünzonen unserer Städte. Gärten, Terrassen, Balkone, Innenhöfe, Parks, Plätze, Straßen und begrünte Gebäude sind einige der Beispiele, die im Folgenden vorgestellt werden. Zudem bietet das Buch zahlreiche Ratschläge zur Gartenplanung und zur großen Vielfalt der Gestaltungsmöglichkeiten von Außenbereichen.

Zweifellos bilden die im Folgenden dargestellten Beispiele einen unschätzbaren Leitfaden für die Wertschätzung dieser wunderbaren grünen Bereiche, die uns umgeben. Die unmittelbare Umgebung schätzen zu lernen, ist die beste Garantie für eine nachhaltige Zukunft, unabhängig davon, ob wir auf dem Land leben oder in der Stadt.

Le jardin constitue aujourd'hui un prolongement de notre maison et nous invite à profiter de l'extérieur. Qu'il s'agisse d'un jardin privé ou d'un parc urbain, il est fondamental de planifier les éléments qui feront partie de cet espace. La liste des espèces végétales, l'importance stratégique de leur répartition et les divers éléments qui contribueront à la création d'un dialogue esthétique (mobilier, éclairage et accessoires) requièrent une bonne organisation afin de pouvoir « vivre » pleinement l'extérieur.

Afin de minimiser l'impact environnemental, il est essentiel de conserver les espaces verts qui apportent de la végétation aux sphères privée et publique de notre habitat. Leur mise en place permet de créer un système d'organismes vivants (plantes, insectes, oiseaux, organismes microscopiques) qui, à son tour, améliore le microclimat de l'environnement en y apportant de l'humidité par le biais des plantes, qui absorbent le CO_2 et fournissent de l'O_2. D'autre part, d'un point de vue personnel, disposer d'un espace avec de la végétation contribue à améliorer l'esthétique du jardin, qui devient un véritable plaisir. Cela permet non seulement de rester en contact avec la nature et d'en faire l'apprentissage, mais également d'ajouter des couleurs, des sons et des odeurs qui stimulent nos sens.

La prolifération actuelle des jardins et potagers urbains participe au développement durable de nos villes, grâce à une production véritablement écologique, qui ne pollue pas et ne dégrade pas l'environnement. Cultiver un balcon aromatique, par exemple, est facile et très pratique puisqu'il fournit des aliments qui n'ont pas été exposés aux produits chimiques de l'agriculture conventionnelle. Qu'il s'agisse de légumes, de tubercules ou encore de plantes aromatiques, le résultat sera toujours le fruit de la motivation, du soin et des efforts consacrés.

D'autre part, de nombreuses initiatives internationales aspirent à la mise en place de systèmes écologiques viables. Les Green Guerrilla, par exemple, travaillent à créer des jardins communautaires sur des terrains abandonnés ou des parcelles inactives en haut des gratte-ciel. La fondation Earth Pledge, quant à elle, propose de recouvrir de vert tous les toits de New York, grâce au programme *Green Roofs,* une belle façon d'alléger la tension du paysage urbain.

Cet ouvrage propose une sélection des espaces verts qui nous entourent, en commençant par nos propres logements pour poursuivre avec ceux qui font partie de nos villes. Jardins, terrasses, balcons, cours intérieures, parcs, places, avenues, bâtiments verts... sont autant d'exemples présentés dans ce livre. De plus, vous y trouverez de nombreux conseils pour organiser votre jardin, avec un large éventail de possibilités en matière d'espaces extérieurs.

Les exemples exposés ici forment sans aucun doute un guide inestimable qui vous permettra d'apprécier ces beaux espaces verts qui nous entourent. Apprendre à estimer notre environnement immédiat est la meilleure garantie d'un avenir durable, que nous vivions à la campagne ou en ville.

Tuinen veranderen in een verlengstuk van onze huizen en nodigen uit om van het buitenleven te genieten. Hetzij in een privé-tuin, hetzij in een stadspark; een planning van de elementen die deel uitmaken van deze ruimte is nodig. De lijst met plantensoorten, het strategische belang van de indeling daarvan en de elementen die een esthetische dialoog teweegbrengen (meubilair, verlichting en accessoires) vereisen een goede organisatie om optimaal van buiten te genieten.

Voor een minimale impact op het milieu is het belangrijk om de begroeide ruimtes die de privé- en openbare sfeer van onze habitat vormen groen te houden. Met de invoering van groene soorten is een habitat van levende organismen gecreëerd (planten, insecten, vogels, microscopische organismen) die op hun beurt het microklimaat verbeteren dankzij de vochtbijdrage van planten, die CO_2 absorberen en O_2 leveren. Op persoonlijk vlak leidt een mooi ingerichte tuin tot puur genot. Het stelt ons niet alleen in de gelegenheid om met de natuur in contact te komen en van haar te leren, maar het schenkt ons bovendien kleuren, geuren en geluiden die onze zintuigen prikkelen.

Tegenwoordig dragen de in opkomst zijnde tuinen en stadsmoestuinen bij aan de duurzaamheid van onze steden. Een zo milieuvriendelijk mogelijke productie vervuilt noch degradeert het milieu. Het verbouwen van groente op een balkon is bijvoorbeeld heel eenvoudig en zeer bevredigend, omdat er geen gebruik wordt gemaakt van de chemische middelen van de conventionele landbouw. Van tuinbouwproducten en knollen tot aromatische planten, het resultaat komt altijd voort uit motivatie, zorg en inspanning.

Daarnaast zijn er talrijke internationale initiatieven om dit ecologische, levensvatbare systeem ten uitvoer te brengen. Zo werkt de Green Guerrilla eraan om gemeenschappelijke tuinen aan te leggen op braakliggend terrein of ongebruikte percelen of helemaal bovenop wolkenkrabbers. De Earth Pledge Stichting is voornemens is om de daken van New York groen te maken met een programma genaamd *Green Roofs*; een prachtige manier om de druk op het stedelijke landschap te verminderen.

Dit boek presenteert een selectie groene ruimtes die ons omringen, te beginnen bij onze eigen woningen en verder tot aan de begroeide ruimtes die onze steden vorm geven. Tuinen, terrassen, balkons, binnenplaatsen, parken, pleinen, lanen en begroeide gebouwen zijn enkele van de voorbeelden die hieronder worden besproken. Het boek biedt bovendien talrijke tips voor de inrichting van de tuin, waarbij een waaier wordt geopend naar alle mogelijke buitenverblijven.

De voorbeelden die hieronder uiteen worden gezet zijn zonder enige twijfel een leidraad van onschatbare waarde voor het waarderen van deze fraaie groene ruimtes die ons omringen. Het leren om de onmiddellijke omgeving te waarderen is de beste garantie voor een duurzame toekomst, of we nu op het platteland of in de stad leven.

I giardini diventano il prolungamento delle nostre case invitandoci a godere degli spazi esterni. Sia in un giardino privato che in un parco urbano è necessaria la pianificazione degli elementi che formeranno parte di detto spazio. La lista delle specie vegetali, l'importanza strategica della loro distribuzione e gli elementi che creeranno un dialogo estetico (mobili, illuminazione e accessori) richiedono una buona organizzazione per poter vivere appieno lo spazio esterno.

Mantenere gli spazi verdi che fanno parte della sfera privata e pubblica del nostro habitat con vegetazione, è imprescindibile per minimizzare l'impatto ambientale. Con la creazione di spazi verdi si dà vita ad un habitat di organismi vivi (piante, insetti, passeri, organismi microscopici) che, a sua volta, migliora il microclima dell'ambiente circostante grazie all'apporto di umidità delle piante che assorbono CO_2 e forniscono O_2. D'altra parte, dal punto di vista personale, disporre di uno spazio verde, migliora esteticamente la casa dandoci piacere, infatti, oltre a permetterci di stare a contatto con la natura, dalla quale apprendiamo un'infinità di cose, ci regala colori, odori e suoni che stimolano i nostri sensi.

Attualmente, la proliferazione di giardini ed orti urbani contribuisce alla sostenibilità delle nostre città. Non vi è dubbio che quanto più ecologica è la produzione, tanto meno contaminiamo e degradiamo l'ambiente. Coltivare un balcone commestibile, per esempio, è semplice ed molto gratificante in quanto ci apporta alimenti che non sono stati esposti ai prodotti chimici dell'agricoltura convenzionale. Sia che si tratti di ortaggi, di tubercoli o di piante aromatiche, il risultato sarà sempre frutto della motivazione, la cura e lo sforzo personale.

D'altra parte esistono numerose iniziative internazionali per l'implementazione di sistemi viabili dal punto di vista ecologico. I Green Guerrilla, per esempio, lavorano per creare giardini comunitari in terreni abbandonati o parcelle inattive dall'alto dei grattacieli. La Fondazione Earth Pledge, invece, si è riproposta di rivestire di verde i tetti di New York, con un programma denominato *Tetti Verdi*, come una maniera di dare sollievo alla pressione del paesaggio urbano.

Questo libro presenta una selezione degli spazi verdi che ci circondano, iniziando dalle nostre stesse abitazioni per continuare con gli spazi verdi che configurano le nostre città. Giardini, terrazze, balconi, cortili interni, parchi, piazze, viali, edifici ricoperti di piante, sono alcuni degli esempi presentati di seguito. Il libro, inoltre, offre numerosi consigli per pianificare il giardino, aprendo un ventaglio di possibilità adattabili a tutti gli spazi esterni.

Non vi è dubbio che gli esempi presentati costituiscano una guida d'inestimabile valore che ci permetterà di apprezzare la bellezza degli spazi verdi che ci circondano: imparare ad apprezzare l'ambiente circostante è la migliore garanzia per un futuro sostenibile sia che si viva in campagna che in città.

Los jardines se convierten en la prolongación de nuestras casas y nos invitan a disfrutar del exterior. Ya sea en un jardín privado o en un parque urbano, la planificación de los elementos que formarán parte de este espacio es un requisito fundamental. La lista de especies vegetales, la importancia estratégica de su distribución y los elementos que crearán un diálogo estético (mobiliario, iluminación y accesorios) necesitan de una buena organización para poder disfrutar plenamente de la vida al exterior.

Cuidar los espacios verdes que conforman la esfera privada y pública de nuestro hábitat es imprescindible para minimizar el impacto ambiental. Con la implantación de espacios verdes se crea un hábitat de seres vivos (plantas, insectos, pájaros, organismos microscópicos) que a su vez mejora el microclima del entorno gracias a la aportación de humedad de las plantas, que absorben dióxido de carbono y proporcionan oxígeno. Por otro lado, desde el punto de vista personal, disponer de un espacio con vegetación mejora estéticamente la vivienda y nos aporta placer, ya que no sólo nos permite estar en contacto con la naturaleza y aprender de ella, sino que además nos regala colores, olores y sonidos que estimulan nuestros sentidos.

Actualmente, la proliferación de jardines y huertos urbanos contribuye a la sostenibilidad de nuestras ciudades. La producción ha de ser lo más ecológica posible para no contaminar ni degradar el medio ambiente. Cultivar un balcón comestible, por ejemplo, es sencillo y muy satisfactorio, ya que proporciona alimentos que no han sido expuestos a los agentes químicos de la agricultura convencional. Desde hortalizas y tubérculos hasta plantas aromáticas, el resultado siempre será fruto de la motivación, el cuidado y el esfuerzo que se le dedique.

Por otra parte, existen numerosas iniciativas internacionales para llevar a cabo sistemas ecológicamente viables. Los Green Guerrilla, por ejemplo, trabajan para crear jardines comunitarios en solares abandonados o parcelas inactivas desde lo alto de los rascacielos. Mientras que la Fundación Earth Pledge se ha propuesto cubrir de verde los tejados de Nueva York, con un programa denominado *Tejados Verdes*, como una hermosa forma de aliviar la presión del paisaje urbano.

Este libro presenta una selección de los espacios verdes que nos rodean, empezando en nuestras propias viviendas y terminando en las zonas verdes urbanas. Jardines, terrazas, balcones, patios interiores, parques, plazas, avenidas y edificios vegetados son algunos de los ejemplos que se presentan a continuación. Además, el libro ofrece numerosos consejos para planificar el jardín, abriendo el abanico a todos los posibles lugares exteriores.

Sin ninguna duda, los ejemplos expuestos a continuación son una guía inestimable para apreciar esos bellos espacios verdes que nos rodean. Aprender a valorar el entorno inmediato es la mejor garantía para un futuro sostenible, tanto si vivimos en el campo como en la ciudad.

PRIVATE GARDEN

DER EIGENE GARTEN

JARDIN PRIVÉ

PRIVÉ-TUINEN

GIARDINO PRIVATO

JARDÍN PRIVADO

Uses and functions of the garden

Nutzung und Funktionen des Gartens

Usages et fonctions du jardin

Gebruik en functies van de tuin

Usi e funzioni del giardino

Usos y funciones del jardín

The garden as an imitation of the landscape is the fruit of a long history based on direct observation and admiration for nature. With the arrival of warm weather, outdoor life intensifies and what better way to enjoy it than have a garden to improvise a cozy dining room while the season lasts. Functional and comfortable furniture help you make the most of the garden. Swings, sandboxes, teeter-totters, play areas for children, swimming pools, the garden offers a variety of activities. It can also include an area to cultivate one kind or another of horticultural crops and flowers make it more decorative. The benefit is twofold: practical and aesthetic.

The first thing to consider is the climate and microclimate of the lot: light and shade, differences in slopes, prevailing winds, orientation (north, south, east and west). Another aspect to consider before planting is to know the characteristics of the land. Depending on whether it is clayey, poor in organic matter or lime, we can cultivate one kind or another of plant species. Equally important is to take into account the maintenance needs. These approaches give us surprising and rewarding yields as well as being a way to have fun.

Crops range from an urban garden to grow vegetables for consumption, to the cultivation of aromatic plants which are much easier to maintain. There is also a very wide variety of native and feral species covering all the needs in terms of shapes, textures, sizes, colors, climate and soil. Winter gardens are another option for countries with extreme climates. These are usually located in glazed spaces where you can achieve as much light as possible to contribute greatly to a sense of comfort in cold weather and keep plants growing at a higher temperature than the exterior.

Le jardin, en tant qu'imitation du paysage, est le fruit d'une longue histoire basée sur l'observation et l'admiration directes de la nature. Avec l'arrivée de la saison chaude, la vie à l'air libre prend de l'importance et il n'y a pas de meilleur moyen d'utiliser un jardin qu'en y improvisant une salle à manger, dont vous pourrez disposer tout au long de la saison. Un mobilier fonctionnel et confortable vous aidera à profiter au maximum du jardin. Balançoires, bacs à sable, balancelles, zones de jeu pour les enfants, piscines... Le jardin offre une grande variété d'activités.

De plus, il est possible d'y intégrer une zone destinée au potager pour y cultiver des espèces horticoles et y inclure des fleurs afin de le rendre plus décoratif. Il présente alors un double avantage : pratique et esthétique.

La première chose à prendre en compte est le climat et les microclimats de la parcelle : lumière, ombres, différences de relief, vents dominants, orientation (nord, sud, est, ouest). Un autre aspect à considérer avant la plantation est de connaître les caractéristiques du terrain. Selon qu'il est argileux, pauvre en matière organique ou calcaire, vous pourrez cultiver différentes espèces végétales. Il est également important de tenir compte des besoins en entretien. Ces différents aspects contribueront à fournir des résultats surprenants et gratifiants, en plus d'une distraction utile.

Les plantations peuvent aller d'un potager urbain, où l'on cultive des légumes pour sa propre consommation, à la culture de plantes aromatiques, beaucoup plus faciles à faire pousser.

Il existe également une variété d'espèces autochtones et sauvages très vaste répondant à tous les besoins en termes de formes, de textures, d'apparences, de couleurs et s'adaptant au climat et sol.

Une autre option pour les pays aux climats extrêmes est le jardin d'hiver. Celui-ci est généralement vitré, ce qui lui permet de recevoir la meilleure luminosité possible afin de contribuer, en grande partie, à une sensation de bien-être pendant les saisons froides, et de pouvoir continuer à cultiver les plantes avec une température plus élevée qu'à l'extérieur.

Der Garten als Nachahmung der Landschaft hat eine lange Geschichte, die auf der Beobachtung und Bewunderung der Natur beruht. Mit der Ankunft der warmen Jahreszeit wird das Leben im Freien intensiver. Gibt es nichts Besseres als einen Garten, um dort ein gemütliches Esszimmer zu improvisieren, solange die Saison anhält? Funktionelles und bequemes Mobiliar erhöht die Freude am Garten. Mit Schaukeln, Sandkästen, Wippen, Spielplätzen für die Kinder und Schwimmbecken bietet der Garten viele Möglichkeiten für Aktivitäten aller Art. Außerdem kann man einen Bereich, der für den Anbau von Gemüse bestimmt ist, einrichten und Blumen anpflanzen. Das hat sowohl einen praktischen als auch einen ästhetischen Nutzen.

Als Erstes müssen wir das Klima und das Mikroklima der Parzelle berücksichtigen: Licht und Sonne, Höhenunterschiede, vorherrschende Winde, die Ausrichtung (nach Norden, Süden, Osten und Westen). Ein weiterer Aspekt, der vor der Bepflanzung in Betracht zu ziehen ist, ist die Eigenschaft des Bodens. Je nachdem, ob er lehmig, humusarm oder kalkhaltig ist, pflanzen wir die eine oder andere Pflanzenart. Ebenso wichtig ist es, den Pflegeaufwand zu berücksichtigen. Diese Planungen führen zu überraschenden und erfreulichen Ergebnissen, abgesehen davon, dass sie ein nützliches Vergnügen darstellen.

Die Pflanzungen können von einem Kleingarten zum Anbau von Gemüse für den Eigenverbrauch bis zur Kräuterzucht reichen, die viel einfacher zu pflegen ist. Es gibt auch sehr viele verschiedene einheimische und wilde Arten, die alle Erfordernisse in Bezug auf Form, Konsistenz, Haltung, Farbe, Klima und Boden abdecken.

Eine weitere Option für Länder mit extremen Klimaverhältnissen sind die Wintergärten. Dabei handelt es sich normalerweise um verglaste Räume, die so viel Licht wie möglich einlassen, wodurch sie viel zum Wohlbefinden in den kalten Jahreszeiten beitragen und es ermöglichen, unsere Pflanzen bei höheren Temperaturen als im Freien zu züchten.

De tuin als imitatie van het landschap is het resultaat van een lange geschiedenis, gebaseerd op waarneming en directe bewondering voor de natuur. Als de warme periode aanbreekt wordt er meer buiten geleefd en wat is er beter dan een tuin om een gezellige eethoek in te richten zolang het seizoen duurt. Met functioneel en comfortabel meubilair kan men maximaal van de tuin genieten. Schommels, zandbakken, wippen, speelzones voor kinderen, zwembaden... de tuin biedt mogelijkheden voor een keur aan activiteiten. Een gedeelte van de tuin kan als moestuin worden ingericht om groente te verbouwen en bloemen te planten voor meer decoratie. De voordelen zijn tweeledig: praktisch en esthetisch.

Het eerste waar we aan moeten denken is het klimaat en de microklimaten van het perceel: licht en schaduwen, hoogteverschillen, dominante winden en ligging (op het noorden, zuiden, oosten of westen). Ook moeten we, alvorens te planten, weten wat de kenmerken van het terrein zijn. Afhankelijk van of de grond kleihoudend, arm aan organisch materiaal of kalkrijk is, moeten er bepaalde plantensoorten worden verbouwd. Even zo belangrijk is om te denken aan de vereisten voor onderhoud. Een goede aanpak kan leiden tot verrassende en tot dankbaarheid stemmende resultaten, naast dat het een vorm van nuttig vermaak is.

Men kan kiezen voor een stadstuin voor het verbouwen van groente voor eigen gebruik, of voor het kweken van aromatische planten, die veel eenvoudiger te verzorgen zijn. Ook bestaat er een grote verscheidenheid aan autochtone en verwilderde soorten die voldoen aan alle wensen voor wat betreft vormen, texturen, uiterlijk, kleuren, klimaat en grond.

Een andere mogelijkheid voor landen met extreme klimaten zijn wintertuinen. Dat zijn meestal beglaasde ruimtes die zo veel mogelijk licht vangen en in grote mate bijdragen aan een gevoel van welzijn in koude seizoenen. Er kunnen planten worden gehouden op een hogere temperatuur dan buiten.

Il giardino come imitazione del paesaggio è la sintesi di una lunga storia basata sull'osservazione e l'ammirazione diretta della natura. Con l'arrivo della bella stagione, la vita all'aria aperta s'intensifica e non c'è niente di meglio di un giardino per improvvisare un soggiorno accogliente finché dura il caldo. Per sfruttare al massimo il giardino l'ideale è ricorrere a dei mobili funzionali e comodi. Altalene, recinti con sabbia, altalene carosello, zone-gioco per i bambini, piscine, il giardino, insomma, offre una gran varietà d'attività. È possibile inserire, inoltre, una zona destinata all'orto per la coltivazione di specie orticole e aggiungerci fiori per renderla più ornamentale. Il beneficio è doppio: pratico ed estetico.

Il primo fattore di cui tenere conto è il clima ed il microclima del terreno: luci ed ombre, dislivelli, venti predominanti, orientazione (nord, sud, est ed ovest). Altri aspetti importanti di cui tenere conto prima della semina sono senz'altro le proprietà fisiche del terreno. Nei terreni argillosi, poveri di materia organica, o calcarei, è bene coltivare determinate specie vegetali. È altrettanto importante tenere conto delle necessità di manutenzione. La considerazione di questi fattori offre una resa sorprendente e gratificante oltre a rappresentare una sana diversione.

Esistono diversi tipi di coltivazioni, dall'orto urbano per coltivare ortaggi per il consumo privato, alla coltivazione di piante aromatiche che necessitano di poche cure. Esiste, inoltre, una gran varietà di specie autoctone ed inselvatichite in grado di coprire ogni necessità di forme, tessiture, aspetti, colori, clima e terreno.

Un'altra possibilità per i paesi dai climi estremi sono i giardini invernali. Si tratta di spazi vetrati, dove si ottiene la maggiore luminosità possibile, che offrono, in gran misura, sensazioni di benessere nei mesi freddi e permettono di continuare a coltivare le nostre piante a temperature superiori rispetto a quelle esterne.

El jardín como imitación del paisaje es producto de una larga historia basada en la observación y la admiración directa por la naturaleza. Con la llegada del calor, la vida al aire libre se intensifica y qué mejor que disponer de un jardín para improvisar un comedor acogedor mientras dura la temporada. Un mobiliario funcional y cómodo ayudará a disfrutar al máximo del jardín. Columpios, areneros, balancines, zonas de juego para los niños, piscinas...: el jardín ofrece una gran variedad de actividades. Además, se puede incorporar una zona destinada a la huerta para el cultivo de especies hortícolas y plantas florales para hacerlo más ornamental. El beneficio es doble: práctico y estético.

Lo primero que debemos tener en cuenta es el clima y los microclimas de la parcela: luz y sombras, diferencias de relieve, vientos dominantes, orientación (norte, sur, este y oeste). Otro de los aspectos a considerar antes de la plantación es conocer las características del terreno. Dependiendo de si es arcilloso, pobre en materia orgánica o calizo, cultivaremos una u otra especie vegetal. Igual de importante es tener en cuenta las necesidades de mantenimiento. Con estas consideraciones, la jardinería, además de ofrecernos resultados sorprendentes y gratificantes, se convertirá en un divertido entretenimiento.

Las plantaciones pueden ir desde un huerto urbano para cultivar hortalizas para el autoconsumo hasta un jardín de plantas aromáticas mucho más fáciles de cuidar. También existe una variedad de especies autóctonas y silvestres muy amplia, con todo tipo de formas, texturas, tamaños y colores, que se adaptan a los diferentes climas y suelos.

Otra opción para los países de climas extremos son los jardines de invierno. Éstos suelen ser espacios acristalados donde se consigue la mayor luminosidad posible para contribuir, en gran medida, a una sensación de bienestar en épocas frías y seguir cultivando nuestras plantas a mayor temperatura que en el exterior.

Nestled away in a hidden corner, a garden area designed for contemplation next to a bench to rest, sleep or meditate is the perfect setting.

Het is een goed idee om een als tuin aangelegd perceel in te richten als plekje om te overpeinzen, als een beschut hoekje met een bank om te ontspannen, te slapen of te mediteren.

Eine hervorragende Idee ist es, in einer versteckten Ecke einen begrünten Rückzugsort zum Ausruhen, Schlafen oder Meditieren einzurichten.

Una buona idea sarà disporre di una porzione di terra destinata alla contemplazione in un angolino nascosto, vicino a una panchina su cui riposare, dormire o meditare.

Une excellente idée consiste à entretenir une parcelle de jardin destinée à la contemplation dans un endroit dissimulé à côté d'un banc pour se reposer, dormir ou méditer.

Una buena idea es acondicionar, en un rincón escondido, un espacio ajardinado destinado a la contemplación con un banco para descansar, dormir o meditar.

Saint-Rémy-de-Provence, France

The French baroque style propagated large gardens with patterned parterres, fountains, recreational areas, statues, potted plants and ornamental flowers.

Tuinen met grote afmetingen met parterres met tekeningen, fonteinen, zones voor vertier, beelden en bakken met sierbloemen, zijn kenmerkend voor de Franse barok.

Der französische Barock förderte ausgedehnte Gärten mit Blumenbeeten mit Mustern, Brunnen, Vergnügungsbereichen, Statuen und blühenden Topfpflanzen.

Lo stile che ha promosso la moda dei giardini di grandi dimensioni è stato il barocco francese. Fanno la loro comparsa aiuole decorative, fontane, muretti, statue e piante in vaso con fiori ornamentali.

Le style baroque français donna naissance à la construction de jardins de grandes dimensions composés de parterres de fleurs formant des dessins, de fontaines, de zones de détente, de statues et de plantes en pot à fleurs d'ornement.

El barroco francés propició los jardines de grandes dimensiones con parterres con dibujos, fuentes, zonas de esparcimiento, estatuas y plantas de maceta con flores ornamentales.

Girona, Spain (left)

Saint-Rémy-de-Provence, France (right)

Saint-Rémy-de-Provence, France (opposite page)

Ponds are always a symbol of peace and relaxation. The refreshing sound of a fountain will create atmosphere in the garden.

Teiche sind immer ein Symbol für Gelassenheit und Ruhe. Das Rauschen des Wassers in einem Brunnen verleiht dem Garten eine erfrischende Atmosphäre.

Les bassins symbolisent systématiquement la sérénité et la décontraction. Le son d'une fontaine imprégnera l'atmosphère du jardin de son bruit rafraîchissant.

Vijvers zijn altijd een symbool van rust en ontspanning geweest. Het geluid van het klaterende water van een fontein geeft de tuin een frisse ambiance.

I laghetti sono da sempre simbolo di serenità e distensione. L'acqua che scorre da una fontana conferirà al giardino una grande atmosfera grazie al suo suono brioso.

Los estanques siempre son símbolo de serenidad y relajación. El sonido del agua que corre en una fuente conferirá al jardín un ambiente refrescante.

Saint-Rémy-de-Provence, France

Raderschall
Zurich, Switzerland

Plants can be grouped together according to their demand for water, to achieve maximum efficiency. For example, plants that require more water should be planted around the edges of the lawn. Do not place a flowering plant or a plant with buds beside a laurel as it would receive unnecessary excess water.

Planten kunnen worden ingedeeld naar hun waterbehoefte: op die manier wordt een efficiënt waterverbruik bereikt. Aan de randen van het gazon kunnen bijvoorbeeld planten worden neergezet die meer water nodig hebben. Planten met bloemen of knoppen kunnen beter niet vlakbij een laurierboom worden gezet, omdat die anders te veel water krijgt.

Die Pflanzen kann man ihrem Wasserbedarf entsprechend gruppieren: so kann man das Wasser effizient nutzen. An den Rändern des Rasens ist es z.B. zweckmäßig, Arten zu pflanzen, die öfter gegossen werden müssen. Wir setzen keine blühende oder knospende Pflanze in die Nähe eines Lorbeerbaums, weil dieser sonst zu viel Wasser bekommen würde.

Le piante possono essere suddivise a seconda delle loro necessità idriche; in questo modo si otterrà un consumo più efficiente. Ai bordi del prato, ad esempio, si possono collocare le piante che hanno bisogno di più acqua. È bene non posizionare una pianta in fioritura o che abbia già sviluppato i boccioli vicino a un alloro, perché quest'ultimo riceverebbe acqua in eccesso.

Les plantes peuvent être regroupées en fonction de leur besoin en eau, ce qui permet d'exploiter efficacement cette ressource. Par exemple, les plantes gourmandes en eau peuvent être placées en bordure de gazon. Une plante à floraison ou à boutons ne doit pas pousser à côté d'un laurier, car ce dernier sera alors alimenté avec un excès d'eau dont il n'a pas besoin.

Las plantas se pueden agrupar por su demanda de agua: de este modo, se conseguirá un uso eficiente de la misma. Por ejemplo, en los bordes del césped es conveniente situar las especies que necesitan más riego. En cambio, no hay que situar una planta de floración o con capullos junto a un laurel porque este último recibiría demasiada agua.

To achieve a wild garden, plants with bright and colorful flowers or those with large leaves should be placed in the foreground, where you can appreciate the detail. Special plants are also placed in the foreground, as you can use them as a starting point to distribute the other garden plants creating gaps in what otherwise would only be a mass of green confusion. Those with small leaves and flowers will be kept to the back.

Voor een wilde tuin moeten planten met opvallende bloemen of met grote bladeren op de voorgrond worden geplaatst, waar ze in detail kunnen worden bekeken. Planten die we willen laten opvallen komen ook vooraan te staan. Bij de inrichting van de tuin moeten er lege plekken worden opengelaten, om te voorkomen dat er een onduidelijke groene massa ontstaat. Planten met kleine bladeren en bloemen worden gereserveerd voor op de achtergrond.

Für einen wilden Garten werden Pflanzen mit üppigen Blüten oder mit großen Blättern im Vordergrund gesetzt, wo man die Einzelheiten gut sehen kann. Auch Pflanzen, die wir hervorheben möchten, werden in die erste Reihe gesetzt; mit ihnen kann man den Garten aufteilen. Man lässt dabei jedoch Stellen frei, um eine konfuse grüne Masse zu vermeiden. Pflanzen, die kleine Blätter und Blüten haben, sind für den Hintergrund reserviert.

Per ottenere un giardino selvatico, le piante che hanno fiori vistosi o grandi foglie saranno disposte in primo piano, così da rendere immediatamente visibili questi dettagli. Le piante a cui si vuol dare risalto dovranno essere a loro volta collocate in primo piano; queste ultime costituiranno elementi di discontinuità in quella che altrimenti risulterebbe una monotona massa verde. Le piante che presentano foglie e fiori piccoli saranno invece disposte sul letto del giardino.

Pour obtenir un jardin sauvage, les plantes à fleurs voyantes ou celles possédant de grandes feuilles seront placées au premier plan, où l'on peut apprécier les détails. Les plantes spéciales seront aussi semées en première ligne. Celles-ci permettent de distribuer la plantation du jardin en laissant des espaces vierges afin d'éviter la présence d'une masse verte chaotique. Les plantes ornées de fleurs et de feuilles de petite taille seront quant à elles placées en arrière-plan.

Para conseguir un jardín salvaje, las plantas con flores vistosas o las que tengan hojas grandes se colocarán en un primer plano, donde se puedan apreciar los detalles. Las plantas que queramos resaltar se situarán también en primera línea; con ellas se puede distribuir la plantación del jardín dejando espacios vacíos para evitar crear una masa verde confusa. Las que tengan las hojas y flores pequeñas se reservarán para el fondo.

María Ros, Ignacio Poch
Girona, Spain

Dry Design
Santa Mónica, CA, USA
(left and right)

María Ros, Ignacio Poch
Girona, Spain
(opposite page)

Juan Roca Vallejo
Santa Cruz, Costa Rica

Ibiza, Spain

Garden benches should be surrounded by vegetation to create a hidden nook in which to relax. By creating points of attraction it will appear that there are more corners than they really are in the garden. A sculpture, a fountain or simply your favorite plants will set the perfect scene.

Het is raadzaam om tuinbanken te omringen met vegetatie, zodat een afgezonderde relaxruimte ontstaat. Als er verschillende aandachtspunten worden gecreëerd lijkt het alsof er meer hoekjes in de tuin zijn dan werkelijk het geval is. Een beeld, fontein of gewoon uw favoriete planten maken het plaatje helemaal af.

Die Gartenbänke sollten von Vegetation umgeben sein, um einen Rückzugsort zu schaffen, an dem man ausruhen kann. Wenn man mehrere attraktive Stellen gestaltet, wirkt es so, als gäbe es mehr Nischen, als der Garten wirklich hat. Eine Skulptur, ein Brunnen oder einfach Ihre Lieblingspflanzen ergänzen die Szenerie.

Si raccomanda di circondare di vegetazione le panchine al fine di ottenere uno spazio protetto in cui potersi rilassare. Se si creeranno diversi angoli speciali il giardino sembrerà più vivibile e intimo. Una scultura, una fontana o le vostre piante preferite completeranno l'insieme.

Il est conseillé d'entourer les bancs du jardin de végétation pour créer un espace retiré prédisposé à la détente. La formation de points d'attraction donnera la sensation que le jardin renferme davantage de recoins qu'il n'en abrite réellement. Une sculpture, une fontaine ou tout simplement vos plantes préférées viendront compléter la scène.

Se recomienda que los bancos del jardín estén rodeados de vegetación para conseguir un espacio recóndito donde poder relajarse. Si se crean puntos de atracción parecerá que hay más rincones de los que realmente existen en el jardín. Una escultura, una fuente o simplemente tus plantas favoritas completarán la escena.

Shaded areas in the garden that receive some sunshine in the mornings are ideal for plants requiring acid soil. The soil can be acidified with peat or iron sulfate before planting.

Schaduwrijke percelen in de tuin, die 's morgens wat zon vangen, zijn ideaal voor planten die op zure grond gedijen. Vóór het planten kan de grond worden verzuurd met witte turf of ijzersulfaat.

Schattige Bereiche des Gartens mit ein wenig Morgensonne sind ideal für Pflanzen, die einen sauren Boden brauchen. Man kann die Erde vor dem Bepflanzen mit Torf oder Eisensulfat säuern.

Le zone in ombra che beneficiano di infiltrazioni di luce durante la mattina sono ideali per le piante che necessitano di un suolo acido. Prima di metterle a dimora, si può preparare il terreno con torba rossa o solfato di ferro.

Les parcelles du jardin peu illuminées, éclairées par les rayons du soleil dans la matinée, sont idéales pour les plantes nécessitant un sol acide. Il est possible d'acidifier le sol avant de procéder à la plantation en y déposant de la tourbe blonde ou du sulfate de fer.

Las parcelas sombrías del jardín con algo de sol por las mañanas son ideales para aquellas plantas que necesitan un suelo ácido. Se puede acidificar el terreno con turba rubia o sulfato de hierro antes de plantar.

Saint-Rémy-de-Provence, France

Saint-Rémy-de-Provence, France
(left)

Ibiza, Spain
(right)

Tuscany, Italy
(opposite page)

Les Baux-de-Provence, France

A fountain close to trees and a resting place has both a calming and aesthetic effect. Sitting by a fountain and listening to the constant flow of water will inject us with a good dose of calmness.

Een fontein in de buurt van bomen en een rustplekje hebben een kalmerend en tegelijkertijd esthetisch effect. Het is zeer ontspannend om bij een fontein te zitten en te luisteren naar het klaterende water.

Ein Brunnen in der Nähe der Bäume und eines Ruheplatzes hat eine beruhigende und gleichzeitig ästhetische Wirkung. An einem Brunnen zu sitzen und dem stetigen Rauschen des Wassers zuzuhören, ist sehr entspannend.

L'installazione di una fontana vicino agli alberi o in un luogo destinato al relax avrà un effetto riposante ed esteticamente apprezzabile. Basterà sedersi accanto alla fontana e ascoltare il costante fluire dell'acqua per godere di una rinnovata serenità.

Le fait d'aménager une fontaine à proximité des arbres et d'un espace de détente permet de générer un effet à la fois apaisant et esthétique. S'asseoir à côté d'une fontaine et écouter le bruissement permanent de l'eau apportera une bonne dose de tranquillité.

Situar una fuente cerca de los árboles o de una zona de descanso tiene un efecto calmante y estético al mismo tiempo. Sentarse junto a una fuente y escuchar el constante fluir del agua resulta muy relajante.

R. Thomson
Oxford, UK

If you have enough space in your garden, install a pergola. A platform with one or two steps on the floor can be ideal to define an outdoor dining room or simply a place to relax..

Als de grootte van de tuin het toelaat kan er een pergola worden neergezet. Een planken vloer, een of twee treden boven de grond, kan ideaal zijn om een buiteneethoek of simpelweg een ontspanningsruimte te creëren.

Wenn der Garten groß genug ist, kann man eine Pergola errichten. Mit einem Podest ein oder zwei Stufen über dem Boden kann man einen Essplatz im Freien gestalten oder einfach einen Ort zum entspannen.

Se le dimensioni del giardino lo permettono, si può inserire una pergola. Una pedana rialzata di uno o due scalini dal terreno può essere l'ideale per costituire un tavolo da pranzo da esterno o semplicemente uno spazio per rilassarsi.

Si les dimensions du jardin le permettent, il est possible d'y aménager une pergola. Un caillebotis surélevé (une ou deux marches) peut s'avérer idéal pour aménager une zone repas extérieure ou tout simplement un espace pour se détendre.

Si las dimensiones del jardín lo permiten, se puede instalar una pérgola. Una tarima de uno o dos peldaños sobre el suelo puede ser ideal para acondicionar un comedor exterior o simplemente un espacio para relajarse.

You can organize a play area in the garden for children with a sandbox. The area should be shaded and have benches for parents.

In de tuin kan een speelplaats met zandbak voor de kinderen worden ingericht. Zorg voor schaduwzones en banken voor de ouders.

Sie können im Garten einen Spielbereich mit einem Sandkasten für die Kinder einrichten. Sorgen Sie für Schattenplätze und Bänke für die Eltern.

È possibile preparare una zona per i giochi dei bambini con un cassone di sabbia. Disponete anche zone ombreggiate e panchine per i genitori.

Vous pouvez aménager une zone de jeu dans le jardin pour les enfants avec un bac à sable. Créez des zones ombragées et disposez des bancs pour les parents.

Puedes habilitar una zona de juego en el jardín para los niños con un arenero. Proporciona también zonas sombreadas y bancos para los padres.

Punta del Este, Uruguay
(opposite page)

dosAdos Arquitectura del Paisaje
Tiana, Spain

CCS Architecture
Sonoma, CA, USA
(opposite page)

The layout of the garden, such as an outdoor dining area, is very important, especially if you have to make maximum use of available space. Give thought to what you need and where to place the furniture.

De indeling van de elementen van de tuin, zoals een eethoek buiten, is erg belangrijk, vooral als het oppervlak maximaal moet worden benut. Het is van wezenlijk belang om te bedenken wat er nodig is en waar de meubels moeten komen te staan.

Die Aufteilung des Gartens in verschiedene Funktionsbereiche, wie z.B. ein Essplatz im Freien, ist sehr wichtig, vor allem, wenn man seine Größe voll ausnutzen will. Sie müssen unbedingt gut darüber nachdenken, was Sie brauchen und wo Sie die Möbel aufstellen.

La disposizione dei giusti elementi nel giardino, come per esempio un tavolo da pranzo, è molto importante, specie se c'è la necessità di sfruttare al massimo la metratura. È essenziale pensare bene a ciò di cui si ha bisogno e a dove andranno posizionati i mobili.

L'agencement du jardin, comme par exemple l'aménagement d'une zone repas, est très important, surtout lorsque les mètres carrés doivent être exploités au maximum. Il s'avère indispensable de bien réfléchir aux besoins et à l'emplacement des meubles.

La distribución de los elementos del jardín, como por ejemplo un comedor exterior, es muy importante, sobre todo si hay que aprovechar al máximo los metros cuadrados. Es imprescindible pensar bien lo que necesitas y donde ubicarás los muebles.

There are many designer collections to give your terrace or garden an air of sophistication, as if it were a room to enjoy the summer. A sofa and coffee table are the perfect accessories for this outdoors living area.

Er zijn talloze ontwerpcollecties die het terras of de tuin een verfijnd tintje geven, als ware het een zitkamer om in de zomer van te genieten. Een bank en een bijzettafel zijn de bondgenoten voor dit terras.

Es gibt sehr viele Designer-Kollektionen, um Ihrer Terrasse oder Ihrem Garten ein raffiniertes Flair zu verleihen, so, als ob es sich um ein Wohnzimmer für den Sommer handeln würde. Ein Sofa und ein Beistelltisch sind die Verbündeten für diesen Bereich im Freien.

Esistono molteplici collezioni di design per dare alla vostra terrazza o al giardino un'atmosfera ricercata, come se fosse un soggiorno in cui godere dell'estate. Un divano e un tavolo d'appoggio saranno un comodo supporto per questa zona giorno all'aria aperta.

De nombreuses collections sont disponibles pour donner à votre terrasse ou jardin un air sophistiqué, comme s'il s'agissait d'un salon pour profiter de l'été. Un canapé et une table auxiliaire seront les alliés de cette zone de vie de plein air.

Existen múltiples colecciones de diseño para dar a tu terraza o jardín un aire de sofisticación, como si se tratara de un salón para disfrutar en verano. Un sofá y una mesa auxiliar serán los aliados para esta zona de estar al aire libre.

RCR Arquitectes
Barcelona, Spain
(opposite page)

To take full advantage of the views place elements close to the viewpoint from which you can enjoy the relaxing sunsets.

Um die Aussicht zu nutzen, sollten Einrichtungsgegenstände in der Nähe des Aussichtsplatzes bereit stehen, von denen man aus entspannt den Sonnenuntergang genießen kann.

Pour exploiter au maximum les vues, disposez des éléments à proximité du point de vue depuis lequel vous pourrez profiter des fins de journée relaxantes.

Om optimaal gebruik te maken van het uitzicht moeten de elementen worden gerangschikt rond het uitzichtspunt van waaruit men kan genieten van ontspannen avonden.

Per godere del panorama disponete gli elementi vicino a un punto panoramico dal quale ammirare rilassanti tramonti.

Para sacar partido de las vistas dispón los elementos cerca del mirador desde donde disfrutar de relajantes puestas de sol.

A sunlounger is ideal for enjoying the garden in spring and summer. Try to install a canopy or umbrella to protect you from the sun's harmful UV rays.

Een ligstoel is ideaal om in de lente en zomer in de tuin te genieten. Probeer om een zonnescherm of parasol in te buurt te hebben, ter bescherming tegen de huidschadelijke UV-stralen van de zon.

Eine Gartenliege ist ideal, um den Garten im Frühling und im Sommer zu genießen. Sorgen Sie dafür, dass sich eine Markise oder einen Sonnenschirm in der Nähe befindet, um Sie vor den UV-Strahlen der Sonne, die so schädlich für die Haut sind, zu schützen.

Una sdraio è l'ideale per godere del giardino in primavera e in estate. Fate in modo di disporla vicino a una tenda da esterni o a un ombrellone per proteggervi dai raggi UV, assai dannosi per la pelle.

Un transat est un élément idéal pour profiter du jardin au printemps et en été. Faites en sorte de le placer à proximité d'un store ou d'un parasol pour vous protéger des rayons UV nuisibles pour la peau.

Una tumbona es ideal para disfrutar del jardín en primavera y en verano. Intenta tener cerca un toldo o una sombrilla para protegerte de los rayos ultravioleta del sol, tan dañinos para la piel.

Ian Chee & Voon Wong

Magín Ruiz de Albornoz
Valencia, Spain
(opposite page)

The design attracts the sun. The originality of exterior furniture allows your time outdoors to be a total luxury. Avant-garde sunloungers and sofas with pure lines are all the rage.

Das Design nimmt ein Sonnenbad. Die Originalität der Gartenmöbel machen die Aufenthalte an der frischen Luft zum Luxus. Schlichte und avantgardistische Gartenliegen und Sofas liegen im Trend.

Le design prend le soleil. L'originalité du mobilier extérieur permet aux escapades à l'air libre de se convertir en véritable luxe. Transats et canapés aux lignes pures et avant-gardistes font partie de la tendance actuelle.

Een ontwerp voor de zon. Dankzij originele tuinmeubels verandert het buitenleven in een luxe. Ligstoelen en banken met strakke, moderne lijnen zijn de heersende trend.

Il design si sdraia a prendere il sole. L'originalità dell'arredamento per esterni rende esclusive le piccole fughe all'aria aperta. La tendenza è per sdraio e divani dalle linee pure e d'avanguardia.

El diseño toma el sol. La originalidad del mobiliario exterior permite que las escapadas al aire libre sean un lujo. Tumbonas y sofás de líneas puras y de vanguardia son la tendencia.

Arborètum
Barcelona, Spain

Try to keep the play area close to the house so that children are supervised at all times. Sand is a must in the space designated for the children's play area. They love digging and building castles.

Legen Sie den Spielplatz möglichst in der Nähe des Hauses an, damit Sie die Kinder jederzeit sehen können. In dem für den Spielplatz bestimmten Bereich ist ein Sandkasten unentbehrlich. Die Kinder lieben es, zu graben und Sandburgen zu bauen.

Faites en sorte que la zone de jeux se trouve à proximité de la maison pour avoir un œil sur les enfants à tout moment. L'espace de jeux doit impérativement posséder un bac à sable. Les enfants adorent creuser et faire des châteaux.

Zorg ervoor dat de speelplaats dichtbij het huis ligt, zodat de kinderen altijd in de gaten kunnen worden gehouden. Zand is onmisbaar voor een speeltuin. Kinderen zijn dol op graven en zandkastelen bouwen.

Fate in modo che la zona gioco sia vicino alla casa per poterla sorvegliare in ogni momento. È imprescindibile che lo spazio che sarà destinato ai giochi dei bambini abbia una zona sabbiosa. Si divertiranno un mondo a scavare e a costruire castelli.

Intenta que la zona de juegos esté cerca de la casa para poder vigilar a los niños en todo momento. En el espacio que destines a zona de juegos la arena es imprescindible. Les encanta cavar y construir castillos.

Habitus Architects
Victoria, Australia

Patrick Clifford, Bowes Clifford Thomson
Medlands Beach, Gran Barrier Island, New Zealand
(right)

Girona, Spain
(opposite page)

If planting a vegetable patch, you must know which crops are better adapted to the climate and soil. If you choose to plant fruit trees you will need to know if they require cross-pollination, that is, if they need the presence of other specimens nearby to pollinate them or if they can bear fruit alone.

Bij het inzaaien van een moestuin moet men weten welke gewassen zich het beste aanpassen aan het klimaat en het terrein. Als er gekozen worden voor fruitbomen, dan is het handig om te weten of er kruisbestuiving nodig is, dat wil zeggen, of het voor de verstuiving nodig is dat er andere exemplaren in de buurt zijn.

Wenn man einen Gemüsegarten anlegen will, kommt es darauf an, welche Sorten am besten für das Klima und den Boden geeignet sind. Wenn man sich für Obstbäume entscheidet, muss man wissen, ob diese Fremdbefruchtung brauchen, d.h., ob andere Exemplare in der Nähe sein müssen, oder ob sie sich allein befruchten können.

Se si semina un orto occorre sapere quali ortaggi sono più adatti al clima e al terreno. Dopo aver scelto gli alberi da frutto sarà necessario sapere se si tratta di specie a impollinazione incrociata, ossia se serve la presenza di altri esemplari nelle vicinanze perché possano impollinarsi o se hanno la capacità di fruttificare da soli.

Avant de planter un potager, il importe de connaître les espèces qui s'adaptent le mieux au climat et au sol. Si le choix se porte sur des arbres fruitiers, il conviendra de savoir si ces derniers requièrent une pollinisation croisée, à savoir si la présence d'autres spécimens plantés à proximité s'avère nécessaire pour les polliniser ou si ces arbres peuvent fructifier sans aide extérieure.

Si se siembra un huerto hay que saber qué cultivos se adaptan mejor al clima y al terreno. Si se opta por árboles frutales conviene saber si requieren polinización cruzada, es decir, si necesitan la presencia de otros ejemplares cercanos para polinizarse o si pueden fructificar solos.

Cactus and succulent plants are common in gardens in a warm climate. They look particularly good in rock gardens with the ground covered with gravel or dry land.

In tuinen in een gematigd/warm klimaat worden cactussen en vetplanten veel gebruikt. Ze zijn ideaal voor steenachtige grond, bedekt met kiezels of onvruchtbare grond.

In Gärten mit einem warmen oder heißen Klima sind Kakteen und Sukkulenten sehr verbreitet. Sie sind für Steingärten mit trockenen Böden oder mit Kies- oder Schotterbelag zu empfehlen.

In luoghi dal clima temperato-caldo è assai comune la messa a dimora di cactus e succulente. È consigliabile disporle in composizioni su suolo coperto di ghiaia o su terra arida.

La plantation de cactus et de crassulacées est couramment rencontrée dans les jardins exposés à des climats tempérés ou chauds. Ces espèces sont conseillées sur les rocailles reposant sur des sols recouverts de gravier ou de terre aride.

Es muy común la plantación de cactus y crasas en jardines de clima templado-cálido. Son aconsejables en rocallas con el suelo cubierto de grava o tierra árida.

Marmol Radziner & Associates
(opposite page)

Fruit trees can be bought from specialist nurseries. If impatience gets the better of you and want the fruit earlier, purchase trees over three years old. Potted trees can be planted all year round, whereas if they are bare root plants, they must be planted in fall or winter.

Fruitbomen zijn verkrijgbaar bij gespecialiseerde kwekerijen. Bent u ongeduldig en wilt u zo snel mogelijk vruchten plukken, koop dan bomen van drie jaar of ouder. Bomen in potten kunnen het hele jaar door worden geplant, terwijl die met een blote wortel alleen in de herfst of winter kunnen worden geplant.

Obstbäume kann man in spezialisierten Baumschulen kaufen. Wenn Sie ungeduldig sind und das Obst so früh wie möglich ernten möchten, kaufen Sie Bäume, die drei Jahre oder älter sind. Eingetopfte Bäume kann man das ganze Jahr über pflanzen, während diejenigen mit nackten Wurzeln unbedingt im Herbst oder Winter eingesetzt werden müssen.

Potete acquistare gli alberi da frutto in vivai specializzati. Se siete impazienti e desiderate cogliere i frutti dei vostri alberi quanto prima, fate in modo che abbiano almeno 3 anni. Gli alberi in vaso possono essere messi a dimora durante tutto l'anno, mentre quelli a radice nuda devono obbligatoriamente essere piantati in autunno o in inverno.

Les arbres fruitiers peuvent être achetés dans des pépinières spécialisées. Si vous êtes de nature impatiente et que vous souhaitez obtenir des fruits le plus tôt possible, achetez des arbres de 3 ans ou plus. Les arbres en pot peuvent être plantés tout au long de l'année, tandis que les arbres à racines nues doivent obligatoirement être plantés en automne ou en hiver.

Los árboles frutales pueden adquirirse en viveros especializados. Si eres impaciente y quieres obtener el fruto cuánto antes, compra árboles de tres años o más. Los árboles en maceta se pueden plantar durante todo el año, mientras que si son a raíz desnuda deben plantarse obligatoriamente en otoño o en invierno.

Arborètum
Barcelona, Spain

In shady locations opt for ground cover plants that cover the ground instead of grass. You can also spread a layer of gravel.

An dunklen Platzen wählen Sie Kriechpflanzen, die den Boden anstelle eines Rasens bedecken. Man kann diese Bereiche auch mit einer Kiesschicht bedecken.

Dans les espaces ombragés, il est préférable d'opter pour des plantes couvre-sol au lieu de gazon. Il est également possible de tapisser le sol d'une couche de gravier.

Kies voor schaduwrijke plekken in plaats van gazon, voor bodembedekkende planten. Een kiezellaag uitspreiden kan ook.

Nelle zone ombreggiate scegliete piante tappezzanti che ricoprano il suolo in alternativa al prato. È anche possibile stendere uno strato di ghiaia.

En los sitios umbríos opta por plantas tapizantes que cubran el suelo en lugar de césped. También se puede extender una capa de grava.

Shrubs can be used to isolate exterior noise and to protect from the wind and they are an effective way to separate zones in the garden. They are also a haven for wildlife like different insects, birds and mammals.

Dicht gesetzte Sträucher sind sehr wirkungsvoll, um den Garten zu unterteilen, und dienen als Sicht-, Lärm- und Windschutz. Außerdem bilden sie einen idealen Lebensraum für Insekten, Vögel und verschiedene Säugetiere.

Les arbustes, agencés en haies et en bosquets, sont très efficaces pour les jardins que l'on souhaite diviser en zones, isoler de l'extérieur et du bruit ou protéger du vent. En outre, ils constituent un abri idéal pour la faune telle que les insectes, les oiseaux ou les mammifères en tout genre.

Struiken die geplant zijn als groep zijn heel efficiënt in tuinen waarin men zones van elkaar of van de buitenwereld wil afscheiden, voor geluidsisolatie en als beschutting tegen de wind. Ze zijn bovendien een ideale schuilplaats voor insecten, vogels en verschillende zoogdieren.

Gli arbusti, messi a dimora come masse arbustive, sono molto efficaci per i giardini nei quali ci si propone di separare zone diverse, isolare rispetto all'esterno o dal rumore e proteggere dal vento. Sono inoltre un rifugio ideale per animali quali insetti, uccelli e diversi mammiferi.

Los arbustos, plantados como masas arbustivas, son muy eficaces en jardines en los que se busca separar distintas zonas, aislar del exterior, del ruido y proteger del viento. Además, son un refugio ideal para los insectos, los pájaros y distintos mamíferos.

Use a potted tree, a statue or fountain to counterbalance a right angle in the garden.

Als de tuin op een recht vierkant lijkt, kan er een boom in een pot, een standbeeld of een fontein worden neergezet, om dit effect te neutraliseren.

Wenn es im Garten rechte Winkel gibt, empfiehlt es sich, einen Blumentopf mit einem Baum, eine Statue oder einen Brunnen aufzustellen, um diese zu neutralisieren.

Se intorno al giardino compare un angolo retto conviene collocare un vaso con un albero, una statua o una fontana per neutralizzarlo.

Il convient de neutraliser toute présence d'angle droit dans le jardin en y plaçant un pot contenant un arbre, une statue ou une fontaine.

Contrarresta el ángulo recto de un jardín colocando una maceta con un árbol, una estatua o una fuente.

Some characteristic elements of the Japanese garden are ponds with fish, lanterns, bridges and wooden furniture. Gazebos invite you to rest along the way and enjoy the landscape, where there is a predominance of tropical vegetation.

Zu den charakteristischen Elementen eines japanischen Gartens gehören Fischteiche, Lampions, Brücken e Mobiliar aus Holz. Pavillons laden zum Verweilen ein, um die tropische Landschaft zu betrachten.

Quelques-uns des éléments caractéristiques du jardin japonais sont les bassins à poissons, les lampions, les ponts et le mobilier en bois. Les tonnelles invitent à faire des pauses en chemin pour contempler le paysage dominé par la végétation tropicale.

Enkele kenmerkende elementen van Japanse tuinen zijn vijvers met vissen, lampions, bruggen en houten tuinmeubels. Prieeltjes nodigen uit om onderweg te stoppen om het landschap met overheersend tropische begroeiing te aanschouwen.

Alcuni degli elementi caratteristici del giardino giapponese sono i laghetti con i pesci, le lanterne, i ponti e l'arredamento in legno. I gazebo invitano a fermarsi lungo il percorso per contemplare il paesaggio, dove predomina una vegetazione lussureggiante.

Algunos de los elementos característicos del jardín japonés son los estanques con peces, los farolillos, los puentes y el mobiliario de madera. Los gacebos invitan a realizar paradas en el camino para contemplar el paisaje, donde predomina la vegetación tropical.

This bridge made entirely from the wood of some old railroad tracks enables us to cross over the pond.

Über eine Brücke, die ganz aus dem Holz alter Schienenschwellen gebaut wurde, kann man den Teich überqueren.

Un pont entièrement fabriqué avec du bois issu d'anciennes voies ferrées permet de traverser le bassin.

Via een brug, die helemaal gemaakt is van oude spoorbielzen, kan men de vijver oversteken.

Un ponte realizzato interamente con il legno di antiche traversine ferroviarie permette di transitare su uno stagno.

Un puente realizado enteramente con la madera de unas antiguas vías de tren permite transitar por encima del estanque.

Aquatic plants, craftwork and traditional sculptures decorate the ponds surrounding the residences. The porch is an ideal space in which to appreciate large leafy plants and fruit trees.

Wasserpflanzen, Kunsthandwerk und traditionelle Skulpturen schmücken die Teiche in der Umgebung der Wohnhäuser. Von der Veranda aus kann man die großblättrigen Pflanzen und Obstbäume betrachten.

Plantes aquatiques, éléments artisanaux et sculptures traditionnelles décorent les bassins qui entourent les résidences. Le porche est un espace idéal pour pouvoir contempler les plantes arborant de grandes feuilles et les arbres fruitiers.

Waterplanten, ambachtswerk en traditionele beelden vormen de decoratie van de vijvers die de woningen omringen. De veranda is een ideale plaats om planten met grote bladeren en fruitbomen te bekijken.

Piante acquatiche, artigianato e sculture tradizionali adornano i laghetti che circondano la residenza. Il portico è lo spazio ideale da cui contemplare latifoglie e alberi da frutto.

Plantas acuáticas, piezas de artesanía y esculturas tradicionales decoran los estanques que rodean las residencias. El porche es un espacio ideal donde poder apreciar las plantas de grandes hojas y los árboles frutales.

Paths enable you to stroll among the plants and according to how they are laid out endorse the flow of the chi. They should be gently winding. A straight path would make the chi flow too fast without any other benefits.

Auf den Pfaden, die durch ihre Form das Fließen des Chi fördern, kann man zwischen den Pflanzen umhergehen. Die Pfade sollten sanft gewunden sein. Ein gerader Pfad würde das Chi zu schnell fließen lassen, ohne Nutzen zu bringen.

Les sentier permettront de se promener entre les plantes et, en fonction de leur forme, favoriseront le flux du Chi. Il est préférable que leurs courbes soient douces. Un sentier rectiligne provoque un flux excessivement rapide du Chi et n'apporte aucun bienfait.

Via de paden kan men tussen de planten doorlopen. Afhankelijk van de vorm bevorderen ze de chi-stroom. Ze hebben bij voorkeur zachte bochten. Door een recht pad stroomt de chi te snel, zonder dat men ervan kan profiteren.

I sentieri consentiranno di passeggiare tra le piante e in funzione della forma scelta favoriranno il flusso del qi. È consigliabile un disegno con curve dolci. Un sentiero rettilineo farà fluire il qi troppo rapidamente, impedendo di ottenere benefici.

Los senderos permiten pasear entre las plantas y, según su forma, favorecen el flujo de la energía o *chi*. Es recomendable que tengan curvas suaves. Un camino recto haría fluir el *chi* demasiado rápido sin producir beneficios.

Although flowers in Japanese gardens are not common, it has not always been rare to find them in this type of scenario. During the Heian period (794-1185) they were planted in spectacular gardens.

Hoewel bloemen niet gebruikelijk zijn in Japanse tuinen, zijn ze niet altijd vreemd geweest in dit soort achtergronden. Tijdens de Heian periode (794-1185) werden ze gebruikt in spectaculaire tuinen.

Normalerweise findet man keine Blumen in japanischen Gärten. Aber das war nicht immer so. In der Heian-Periode (794-1185) wurden sie in spektakulären Gärten angepflanzt.

Anche se non è comune trovare fiori nei giardini giapponesi, non sempre sono stati alieni da questo tipo di scenari. Durante il periodo Heian (794-1185) se ne piantavano in giardini spettacolari.

Même si la présence de fleurs n'est pas commune dans les jardins japonais, cela n'a pas toujours été le cas. À l'époque de Heian (794-1185), elles étaient plantées dans des jardins spectaculaires.

Aunque no es habitual encontrar flores en los jardines japoneses, no siempre han sido ajenas a este tipo de escenarios. Durante el período Heian (794-1185) se plantaban en espectaculares jardines.

A cyme with a soft undulating movement favors the flow of chi. Green represents growth and transmits peace and harmony while easing worried minds.

Een top met een lichte golfbeweging bevordert de chi-stroming. Groen is de kleur van de groei, draagt vrede en harmonie uit en zorgt tevens voor verlichting in drukke geesten.

Eine sanft ansteigende Bergkuppe fördert die Zirkulation des Chi. Grün ist die Farbe des Wachstums, vermittelt Frieden und Harmonie und beruhigt gleichzeitig den viel beschäftigten Geist.

Una sommità dal profilo dolce favorisce la circolazione del qi. Il verde è il colore della crescita e trasmette pace e armonia mentre consola le menti intente.

Une cime légèrement ondulée favorise la circulation du Chi. Le vert est la couleur de la croissance. Il transmet paix et harmonie tout en apaisant les esprits inquiets.

Una cima con una ondulación suave favorece la circulación del *chi*. El verde es el color del crecimiento y transmite paz y armonía, a la vez que despeja la mente de preocupaciones.

Arborètum
Barcelona, Spain
(right)

In recent years, courtyards have gained in functionality and sophistication. They have also been enriched by the contributions of other cultures, such as feng shui, including items like stones and avoiding excessive detail.

De laatste jaren hebben binnenplaatsen gewonnen aan functionaliteit en raffinement. Ze zijn bovendien verrijkt met de inbreng van andere culturen, zoals feng shui, met elementen als stenen, en waarbij een overschot aan details wordt vermeden.

In den letzten Jahren haben die Innenhöfe an Funktionalität und Reiz gewonnen. Zudem werden sie durch den Beitrag anderer Kulturen bereichert, wie Feng Shui, Steine und andere Elemente, wobei jede Übertreibung bei den Details vermieden wird.

Negli ultimi anni, i cortili interni si sono evoluti per funzionalità e raffinatezza. Hanno inoltre tratto ispirazione da svariate culture, come il feng shui, utilizzando le pietre come elementi decorativi ed evitando l'eccesso di dettagli.

Au cours des dernières années, les cours intérieures ont gagné en fonctionnalité et sophistication. En outre, elles ont été enrichies grâce à l'apport d'autres cultures, comme le feng shui, intégrant des éléments comme les pierres et évitant l'excès de détails.

En los últimos años, los patios interiores han ganado en funcionalidad y sofisticación. Además, se han enriquecido con el aporte de otras culturas, como el feng shui, incluyendo elementos como piedras y evitando el exceso de detalles.

One of the best ways to expand the home outwards is to have an interior courtyard that can relax the eye and mind from anywhere in the house.

Eine der besten Arten, das Haus nach außen zu erweitern, ist ein Innenhof, der dazu dient, die Sicht und den Geist von jeder Stelle der Wohnung aus zur Ruhe zu bringen.

L'un des meilleurs moyens d'étendre la maison vers l'extérieur consiste à disposer d'une cour intérieure servant à reposer la vue et l'esprit en tout point de la demeure.

Een van de beste manieren om het huis naar buiten toe uit te breiden is een binnenplaats die dienst doet om het zicht en de geest te ontspannen vanuit ieder willekeurige plaats in de woning.

Uno dei modi migliori per creare un ponte tra la casa e l'ambiente esterno è la realizzazione di un cortile interno, in grado di rallegrare la vista e l'umore da qualsiasi punto dell'abitazione.

Una de las mejores formas de expandir la casa hacia el exterior es disponer de un patio interior que sirva para relajar la vista y la mente desde cualquier punto de la vivienda.

Mamen Domingo & Ernest Ferré Arquitectes
Reus, Spain

Pedro López García
Espinardo, Spain

Pedro López García
Espinardo, Spain
(opposite page, left)

SCDA Architects
Singapur, Singapur
(opposite page, right)

Doors and windows are the most important elements in interior courtyards, and they visually link the interior and exterior of the house.

De deuren en ramen zijn de belangrijkste elementen in binnentuinen, aangezien ze het exterieur en binnen visueel met elkaar verbinden.

Türen und Fenster sind die wichtigsten Elemente der Innenhöfe, da sie den Innen- und Außenbereich des Hauses visuell miteinander verbinden.

Le porte e le finestre sono gli elementi più importanti dei cortili interni, perché integrano visivamente l'interno e l'esterno dell'abitazione.

Les portes et les fenêtres sont les éléments les plus importants des cours intérieures en raison du fait qu'elles unissent visuellement l'intérieur et l'extérieur de la maison.

Las puertas y las ventanas son los elementos más importantes de los patios interiores, ya que unen visualmente el interior con el exterior de la casa.

If the interior space is distributed around one or more courtyards with small wooded gardens, it creates a sense of being close to nature.

Als het interieur wordt ingericht rond een of meerdere binnenplaatsen met tuinen en bomen, geeft dat het gevoel dicht bij de natuur te zijn.

Wenn der Innenraum um einen oder mehrere Innenhöfe mit kleinen baumbestandenen Gärten angeordnet wird, entsteht ein Gefühl von Naturnähe.

Se lo spazio abitato si sviluppa intorno a uno o più cortili dotati di piccoli giardini alberati, la casa sembrerà immersa nella natura.

Si l'espace intérieur est distribué autour d'une ou de plusieurs cours avec de petits jardins arborés, il confère alors une sensation de proximité avec la nature.

Si el espacio interior se distribuye alrededor de uno o más patios con pequeños jardines arbolados, se crea una sensación de proximidad a la naturaleza.

Massimo Sottili
(left)

Studio Associato Falconi
(right)

Carles Gelpí i Arroyo
Barcelona, Spain
(left)

Mamen Domingo & Ernest Ferré Arquitectes
Reus, Spain
(right)

idea of planting a tree in a courtyard has very relative results, depend on the type of tree. The best option is a small es. That's why you must have an idea of the size that trees to when you buy one to assure that you have enough space.

dee om in een binnenplaats een boom te planten, geeft een taat dat afhangt van de gekozen soort. De beste optie is leine boom. Daarom moeten we bij de aankoop al een idee en van de afmetingen die de bomen bereiken, om er zeker e zijn dat ze voldoende ruimte hebben.

Die Wirkung eines Baums in einem Innenhof ist sehr abhängig von der gewählten Art. Am besten ist ein kleiner Baum. Deshalb müssen wir beim Kauf eine Vorstellung davon haben, wie groß die Bäume werden, um zu sehen, ob sie genug Platz haben.

L'idea di piantare un albero in un giardino interno va incontro a esiti diversi, che dipenderanno dal tipo di pianta. È meglio puntare su un albero di piccole dimensioni. Al momento dell'acquisto bisogna quindi avere un'idea precisa delle dimensioni massime raggiungibili dalle varie specie.

La plantation d'un arbre dans une cour intérieure donne des résultats très relatifs qui dépendront de l'espèce choisie. Mieux vaut porter son choix sur un arbre de petite taille. C'est pour cette raison qu'il importe d'avoir une idée des dimensions que peuvent atteindre les arbres avant de les acheter pour s'assurer de la présence d'un espace suffisant.

La idea de plantar un árbol en un patio interior tiene resultados muy relativos en función del tipo de especie elegida. La mejor opción es un árbol pequeño. Por eso debemos tener una idea de los tamaños que alcanzan los árboles a la hora de comprarlos para ver si hay suficiente espacio.

kt & Verdickt Architecten
rp, Belgium

Architects
pur, Singapur
site page)

The lounge and dining room are distributed in an L shape and the courtyard is located in the remaining part, so that it can equally light up both rooms. In the pool area there is considerable interaction between the interior and exterior, offering a view of the surrounding landscape.

De zitkamer en eetkamer zijn in L-vorm ingericht. De binnenplaats ligt in het resterende stuk, zodat beide vertrekken op dezelfde wijze verlicht kunnen worden. Bij het zwembad vindt een opmerkelijke wisselwerking tussen binnen en buiten plaats en vanuit die plaats heeft men uitzicht op het omringende landschap.

Das Wohnzimmer und der Essbereich sind L-förmig angeordnet und der Innenhof befindet sich in dem dazwischen liegenden Platz, so dass er beide Räume gleichmäßig erhellt. Beim Swimmingpool gibt es ein bemerkenswertes Zusammenspiel von innen und außen mit Sicht auf die umgebende Landschaft.

Il salone e la sala da pranzo sono disposti a L e il cortile interno è situato nella parte restante del rettangolo, così da poter illuminare in ugual misura entrambe le stanze. La piscina favorisce la fusione tra interno ed esterno, offrendo un buon punto di osservazione per godere del panorama circostante.

Le salon et la salle à manger sont agencés en forme de L et la cour intérieure est située dans la partie complémentaire, de sorte qu'elle illumine les deux pièces de manière équivalente. La piscine maintient une interaction significative entre l'intérieur et l'extérieur, tout en offrant une vue sur le paysage environnant.

El salón y el comedor están distribuidos en forma de L y el patio interior está situado en la parte restante del rectángulo, de modo que pueda iluminar ambas estancias de igual manera. En la piscina existe una notable interacción entre el interior y el exterior, ofreciendo una vista del paisaje circundante.

brh+
Florence, Italy

Kenji Tagashira
Kizugawa, Japan
(opposite page)

Stones and pebbles surround this wooden and concrete walkway in a space that connects the exterior of the house with its interior.

Steine und Kiesel umgeben diesen Holzsteg aus Holz und Beton in einem Raum, der den Außenbereich des Hauses mit seinem Inneren verbindet.

Pierres et galets entourent cette passerelle en bois et en béton dans un espace unissant l'extérieur de la maison avec son intérieur.

Stenen en kiezelstenen omringen deze houten en betonnen passarelle in een ruimte waar interieur en exterieur met elkaar worden verbonden.

Pietre e ciottoli cingono questa passerella di legno e cemento in uno spazio che unisce esterno e interno dell'abitazione.

Piedras y guijarros rodean esta pasarela de madera y hormigón en un espacio que une el exterior de la casa con su interior.

Cañas Arquitectos
Ocotal, Guanacaste, Costa Rica

Studio Associato Falconi

Junya Toda Architects & Associates
Osaka, Japan
(opposite page)

Hedges are perhaps the most common structural elements of the garden. It is important to know the exact role of each hedge. Shrubs that are trimmed with a rounded appearance should be separated from those that have no specific shape.

Hecken sind vielleicht die häufigsten Strukturelemente des Gartens. Man muss unbedingt wissen, welche Funktion jede Hecke haben soll. Sträucher, die rund geschnitten werden sollen, müssen von denen, die ihre Form behalten, getrennt werden.

Les haies constituent probablement l'élément structurel le plus fréquent dans les jardins. Il s'avère indispensable de connaître la fonction remplie par chaque haie. Les arbustes de forme arrondie doivent être séparés des arbustes conservant une forme non définie.

Omheiningen zijn misschien wel de meest gangbare structurele elementen van de tuin. Het is heel belangrijk om te weten welke functie de omheining moet hebben. Struiken die bestemd zijn om in ronde vormen te worden geknipt moeten gescheiden staan van struiken waarvan de vorm niet precies hoeft te worden bepaald.

Le siepi sono forse il più comune elemento strutturale del giardino. È imprescindibile sapere che funzione avrà ogni siepe. Gli arbusti destinati a essere potati a forma tonda dovranno essere separati da quelli che potranno svilupparsi liberamente.

Los setos constituyen quizás el más común de los elementos estructurales del jardín. Es imprescindible determinar qué función tendrá cada seto. Los arbustos podados con formas redondas deberán separarse de aquellos otros con formas indefinidas.

Arborètum
Barcelona, Spain

Boxwood shrubs look well in corners or to mark a path. Furniture should be chosen based on the space and the use we give to each àrea.

Buksen zijn een goede optie om op hoeken te plaatsen of om een pad af te bakenen. De keuze voor het meubilair is afhankelijk van de ruimte en het gebruik dat aan iedere zone wordt gegeven.

Buchsbaumsträucher sind gut für Ecken geeignet, oder einfach um den Rundweg zu markieren. Die Möblierung richtet sich nach dem vorhanden Platz und dem Gebrauch, dem wir jedem Bereich zuweisen.

Il bosso è una buona scelta come ornamento agli angoli o semplicemente per evidenziare il percorso. L'arredamento sarà scelto in funzione dello spazio e della destinazione d'uso che si darà a ogni area.

Les buis sont une excellente option pour les angles ou tout simplement pour tracer un chemin. Le mobilier sera choisi en fonction de l'espace et de l'usage donné à chaque zone.

Los bojes son una buena opción para colocar en las esquinas o simplemente para marcar el recorrido. El mobiliario se escogerá en función del espacio y el uso que le demos a cada área.

Arborètum
Barcelona, Spain

Arborètum
Barcelona, Spain

All elements must be distributed to scale, depending on the size of the garden. If shrubs or trees are too large, they create too much shade.

Alle elementen moeten op schaal worden gedistribueerd, afhankelijk van de afmetingen van de tuin. Als de struiken of bomen te groot zijn, geven ze teveel schaduw.

Alle Elemente müssen den Dimensionen des Gartens angepasst sein. Wenn die Sträucher oder Bäume zu groß sind, geben sie zu viel Schatten.

Tutti gli elementi devono essere distribuiti in scala, in accordo con le dimensioni del giardino. Se gli arbusti e gli alberi sono troppo grandi, proietteranno ombre eccessive.

Tous les éléments doivent être distribués à l'échelle, en fonction des dimensions du jardin. Des arbustes ou des arbres trop grands sont sources d'ombre excessive.

Todos los elementos deben ser distribuidos a escala, según las dimensiones del jardín. Si los arbustos o los árboles son demasiado grandes, crearán excesiva sombra.

Go for smaller trees, preferably deciduous, for each corner so that the winter sun shines through when the trees lose their leaves.

Kies kleine en bij voorkeur loof verliezende bomen voor iedere hoek, zodat de zon in de winter, als er geen blaadjes zijn, naar binnen kan schijnen.

Wählen Sie für jede Ecke niedrige, laubabwerfende Bäume, damit die Sonne im Winter hineinscheinen kann.

Scegliete alberi di piccolo portamento per ogni angolo, preferendo quelli decidui di modo che la luce del sole possa entrare quando in inverno perderanno le foglie.

Choisissez des arbres de petite taille pour chaque coin du jardin en optant de préférence pour des espèces à feuilles caduques afin que les rayons du soleil puissent pénétrer l'espace en hiver lorsque les arbres sont dénudés.

Escoge árboles de tamaño pequeño para cada esquina y preferentemente de hoja caduca para que el sol entre en invierno cuando pierdan las hojas.

Arborètum
Barcelona, Spain

When buying a tree, make sure it has not been planted in the ground. If so you run the risk that it has not taken root properly in the container. Besides, before planting any tree or shrub you must have an idea of the size it will grow to, in order to control the areas of sun and shade.

Wenn Sie einen Baum oder eine Palme kaufen, vergewissern Sie sich, dass diese nicht im Boden aufgezogen worden sind. In diesem Fall besteht das Risiko, dass sie in dem Gefäß nicht richtig verwurzelt sind. Es ist auch wichtig, vor dem Pflanzen von Bäumen oder Sträuchern eine Vorstellung zu haben, welchen Umfang sie erreichen, um die Sonnen- und Schattenbereiche bestimmen zu können.

Lorsque vous achetez un arbre ou un palmier, veillez à ce que celui-ci n'ait pas été élevé dans le sol. Le cas échéant, il est possible qu'il ne soit pas correctement enraciné dans le récipient. Avant de planter un arbre ou un arbuste, il est indispensable d'avoir une idée du volume que celui-ci occupera en vue de contrôler les zones ensoleillées et ombragées.

Let er bij het kopen van een boom of palmboom op dat ze niet in de aarde zijn gekweekt. Als dat wel zo is, bestaat het risico dat ze niet goed hebben geworteld in de bak. Alvorens een boom of struik over te planten is het eveneens van groot belang om een idee te hebben van hoe groot ze worden, om de zon- en schaduwzones te kunnen controleren.

Nel momento in cui comprate un albero o una palma assicuratevi che la pianta non sia stata cresciuta direttamente nel terreno. In quel caso rischierebbe di non aver radicato correttamente nel contenitore. Inoltre, prima di piantare qualsiasi albero o arbusto è fondamentale avere un'idea del volume che potrà acquisire per progettare le zone di sole e di ombra.

Cuando compres un árbol o una palmera asegúrate de que no haya sido criado en el suelo. Si es así, corremos el riesgo que no haya enraizado correctamente en el contenedor. También, antes de plantar cualquier árbol o arbusto es fundamental tener una idea del volumen que adquirirá para tener controladas las zonas de sol y sombra.

Arborètum
Barcelona, Spain

This terrace has been designed on the basis of simple principles that can be applied to any outdoor space: choose low-maintenance plants, a few species, light and elegant furnishings.

Het ontwerp van dit terras is gebaseerd op enkele heel eenvoudige principes die ook toegepast kunnen worden bij een willekeurige ruimte in de open lucht: kies voor planten die weinig onderhoud nodig hebben, combineer slechts enkele soorten en kies voor licht en elegant meubilair.

Das Design dieser Terrasse beruht auf sehr einfachen Prinzipien, die an jedem beliebigen Ort im Freien funktionieren: Pflanzen, die wenig Pflege brauchen, wenig Artenvielfalt, Licht und elegantes Mobiliar.

Il design di questa terrazza si basa su principi molto semplici, che possono essere adattati a qualsiasi spazio all'aria aperta: la scelta di piante che necessitino poche cure, una limitata varietà, luminosità e arredamento elegante.

La conception de cette terrasse repose sur des principes très simples qui peuvent fonctionner dans n'importe quel espace extérieur : choix de plantes ne nécessitant que peu d'entretien, faible diversité d'espèces, lumière et mobilier élégant.

El diseño de esta terraza se basa en unos principios muy simples que pueden funcionar en cualquier espacio al aire libre: selección de plantas que necesiten poco mantenimiento, poca variedad de especies, luz y mobiliario elegante.

Arborètum
Barcelona, Spain

Arborètum
Barcelona, Spain

Use a pair of key plants to set off a space under a porch or pergola. In this case, the living area is flanked by a palm tree and a cactus.

Plaats een paar in het oog springende planten, die de ruimte onder een galerij of pergola beter doen uitkomen. In dit geval wordt het zitgedeelte geflankeerd door een palmboom en een cactus.

Setzen Sie ein paar auffällige Pflanzen, die den Platz unterhalb einer Veranda oder einer Pergola hervorheben. In diesem Fall wird der Wohnbereich von einer Palme und einem Kaktus flankiert.

Collocate un paio di piante che siano protagoniste dello spazio e costituiscano un porticato o una pergola. In questo caso, la zona-soggiorno è fiancheggiata da una palma e da un cactus.

Placez deux plantes phares mettant en valeur l'espace situé sous un porche ou une pergola. Dans ce cas précis, la zone de vie est flanquée d'un palmier et d'un cactus.

Coloca un par de plantas protagonistas que realcen el espacio bajo un porche o una pérgola. En este caso, la zona de estar está flanqueada por una palmera y un cactus.

Ornamental shrubs are fundamental in the garden. They usually do not grow beyond 10 feet high. Other advantages include their aesthetic quality, as many of them release a pleasant aroma and their leaves may be different shades of green. Some have decorative fruits such as the strawberry tree, the holly or the pomegranate.

Ziersträucher sind eine wichtige Pflanzenart für den Garten. Sie werden normalerweise nicht höher als 3 Meter. Unter anderem zeichnen sie sich durch ihre ästhetische Qualität aus, da viele von ihnen blühen und angenehm duften und ihre Blätter in verschiedenen Grüntönen leuchten. Manche tragen dekorative Früchte wie der Erdbeerbaum, die Stechpalme oder der Granatbaum.

La présence d'arbustes ornementaux est indispensable dans le jardin. Ils possèdent généralement une hauteur inférieure à 3 mètres. Parmi d'autres avantages, ces arbustes se distinguent par leur qualité esthétique. Nombre d'entre eux fleurissent en effet en dégageant un arôme agréable et leurs feuilles peuvent arborer différentes nuances de verts. Certains donnent des fruits décoratifs comme l'arbouse, le houx ou le grenadier.

Ornamentele struiken zijn een fundamentele plantensoort in de tuin. Ze zijn normaal gesproken niet hoger dan 3 meter en hebben onder andere het voordeel dat ze esthetische kwaliteiten hebben. Vele verspreiden tijdens de bloeiperiode een aangename geur en hun bladeren kunnen verschillende groentinten hebben. Enkele soorten, zoals de aardbeiboom, beshulst of granaatappel, dragen decoratieve vruchten

Gli arbusti ornamentali sono un tipo di pianta fondamentale nel giardino. Hanno di solito un'altezza che non supera i 3 m. Tra gli altri aspetti positivi spicca la loro bellezza: molti fioriscono diffondendo un gradevole aroma e le loro foglie possono essere brillanti su diverse tonalità di verde. Alcuni, come il corbezzolo, l'agrifoglio o il melograno, hanno frutti decorativi.

Los arbustos ornamentales son un tipo de planta fundamental en el jardín. Suelen tener una altura que no sobrepasa los 3 metros. Entre otras ventajas, destaca su calidad estética, ya que muchos de ellos florecen desprendiendo un agradable aroma y sus hojas pueden lucir diferentes matices de verdes. Algunos poseen frutos decorativos como el madroño, el acebo o el granado.

Arborètum
Barcelona, Spain

A clump of bushes planted behind a fence will give you more privacy while acting as a barrier against noise and lessening the force of prevailing winds.

Eine Gruppe von Sträuchern hinter einem Zaun bietet Sichtschutz, dämpft den Lärm von draußen und hält starken Wind ab.

Un groupe d'arbustes situés derrière une clôture permettra de protéger l'espace des regards extérieurs, tout en jouant le rôle de barrière contre le bruit et en atténuant la force des vents dominants.

Door een groep struiken achter een hek te plaatsen voorkomt u inkijk, wordt een geluidsbarrière gevormd en wordt de kracht van de dominante winden verminderd.

Un gruppo di arbusti situati oltre uno steccato permetterà di isolare lo spazio dagli sguardi degli estranei; allo stesso tempo, sarà una barriera antirumore e diminuirà l'impeto dei venti dominanti.

Un grupo de arbustos situados tras una valla permitirá mantener aislado el espacio de miradas ajenas a la vez que será una barrera contra el ruido y aminorará la fuerza de los vientos dominantes.

Arborètum
Barcelona, Spain

Prefabricated fountains can be purchased and they can be easily and quickly installed. The most common examples are stone or ceramic made. However, many people are interested in designing their own fountain and then turn to a specialist for advice and the subsequent installation.

Fonteinen zijn geprefabriceerd te koop en kunnen snel en eenvoudig worden geïnstalleerd. De meeste zijn van steen of keramiek. Veel mensen willen echter hun eigen fontein ontwerpen en roepen een deskundige in voor advies en voor het installeren.

Brunnen kann man vorgefertigt kaufen und schnell und einfach installieren. Die am meisten gebrauchten sind aus Stein oder Keramik. Viele Menschen wollen jedoch lieber ihren eigenen Brunnen entwerfen und lassen sich von Fachleuten beraten, die ihn später installieren.

Le fontane possono essere comprate prefabbricate: le più comuni sono in pietra o ceramica. La loro installazione è spesso semplice e rapida, tuttavia molte persone desiderano progettare la propria fontana e affidare a un professionista la consulenza e l'installazione finale.

Des fontaines préfabriquées, rapides et faciles à installer, sont disponibles dans le commerce. Les plus répandues sont en pierre ou en céramique. Toutefois, nombre sont les personnes intéressées à concevoir leur propre fontaine et à faire appel à un spécialiste pour les conseiller et se charger de l'installation.

Las fuentes se pueden comprar prefabricadas, y tienen una instalación rápida y sencilla. Las más comunes son de piedra o cerámica. Sin embargo, a muchas personas les interesa diseñar su propia fuente y dejar en manos del especialista el asesoramiento y su posterior instalación.

Raderschall
Zurich, Switzerland
(this page)

Mallorca, Spain

This country house surrounded by irrigated and garden crops has recovered its original character with great care and sensitivity. The pool is made of natural stone and has respected the surrounding vegetation.

Der ursprüngliche Charakter dieses Gutes, das von Gemüse- und Obstgärten und Bewässerungsanlagen umgeben ist, wurde mit viel Sorgfalt und Sensibilität bewahrt. Der Swimmingpool ist aus Naturstein und die Vegetation der Umgebung wurde erhalten.

Dans cette propriété entourée de cultures irriguées et de vergers, le caractère original du site a été récupéré avec sensibilité et le plus grand soin. La piscine est en pierre naturelle et a été construite en respectant la végétation du milieu.

In dit landhuis, omringd door tuinbouwgewassen en bevloeide grond, is het originele karakter zorgvuldig en met smaak teruggehaald. Het zwembad is van natuursteen en de vegetatie van de omgeving is behouden gebleven.

In questa fattoria circondata da campi sono state recuperate con grande attenzione e sensibilità le caratteristiche originarie del luogo. La piscina è in pietra naturale ed è stata rispettata la vegetazione autoctona.

En esta finca rodeada de cultivos de huerta y regadío se ha recuperado con sumo cuidado y sensibilidad su carácter original. La piscina es de piedra natural y se ha respetado la vegetación del entorno.

Mallorca, Spain

We recommend placing the pond in a shady area, because algae thrive in the sun. Water lilies and floating plants will provide shade to the water surface and will prevent the accumulation of algae.

Het is aan te raden om de vijver in een schaduwrijke zone aan te leggen, aangezien algen van de zon houden. Waterlelies en drijfplanten zorgen voor schaduw op het wateroppervlak en voorkomen de wildgroei van algen.

Es ist ratsam, den Teich in einer Schattenzone anzulegen, da die Algen die Sonne lieben. Seerosen und schwimmende Pflanzen sorgen für Schatten auf dem Wasser und verhindern die Vermehrung von Algen.

Si consiglia di posizionare il laghetto in una zona ombreggiata, visto che le alghe per svilupparsi hanno bisogno di luce. Ninfee e piante galleggianti forniranno ombreggiatura alla superficie dell'acqua ed eviteranno la proliferazione delle alghe.

Il est conseillé d'installer le bassin dans une zone ombragée. Les algues sont en effet avides de soleil. Les nénuphars et les plantes flottantes apporteront de l'ombre à la surface de l'eau et permettront d'éviter la prolifération des algues.

Se aconseja situar el estanque en una zona con sombra, ya que a las algas les gusta el sol. Los nenúfares y las plantas flotantes aportarán sombra a la superficie del agua y evitarán la proliferación de algas.

Faulkner & Chapman Landscape Design
Brighton, Australia
(left)

Raderschall
Zurich, Switzerland
(right)

Dardelet
Winkel, Switzerland
(opposite page, left)

Raderschall
Zurich, Switzerland
(opposite page, right)

Naturalized pools are a prime example of cooperating with the environment. There is no need for any chemical products, as water is kept clean naturally using flora and fauna as purifiers.

Der Natur angepasste Swimmingpools sind ein Beispiel für die Zusammenarbeit mit der Umwelt. Chemische Produkte sind unnötig. Das Wasser wird auf natürliche Weise sauber gehalten, indem als einziges Reinigungsprodukt die Flora und Fauna verwendet wird.

Les piscines naturelles sont un exemple d'interaction avec le milieu. Sans recourir à aucun produit chimique, l'eau conserve son état de propreté de manière naturelle en utilisant la flore et la faune pour seuls épurateurs.

Natuurzwembaden zijn een voorbeeld van de wisselwerking met de omgeving. Het water wordt op natuurlijke wijze schoongehouden, zonder dat daarvoor chemische producten nodig zijn. De flora en fauna worden gebruikt als enige zuiveraars.

Le piscine naturali sono un esempio di interdipendenza con l'ambiente. Senza bisogno di alcun prodotto chimico, l'acqua è mantenuta pulita in modo naturale usando come unici depuratori la flora e la fauna.

Las piscinas naturalizadas son un ejemplo de cooperación con el entorno. Sin necesidad de ningún producto químico, el agua se mantiene limpia de manera natural, usando como únicos depuradores la flora y la fauna.

Mallorca, Spain

Check the pH of the water at least once a week. The pH value should be 7.2 to 7.6. Chlorine will help destroy microorganisms, fungi and bacteria and keep the water clean.

Kontrollieren Sie mindestens ein Mal pro Woche den pH-Wert des Wassers. Der pH-Wert muss zwischen 7,2 und 7,6 liegen. Chlor hilft, Mikroorganismen, Pilze und Bakterien zu zerstören und das Wasser sauber zu halten.

Contrôlez le pH de l'eau au moins une fois par semaine. La valeur du pH doit être comprise entre 7,2 et 7,6. Le chlore favorisera la destruction des micro-organismes, des champignons et des bactéries, tout en permettant de garder l'eau limpide.

Controleer de pH van het water tenminste een keer per week. De pH-waarde moet tussen 7,2 en 7,6 liggen. Chloor helpt mee om micro-organismen, schimmels en bacteriën te doden en om het water schoon te houden.

Controllate il pH dell'acqua almeno una volta alla settimana. Il valore deve essere compreso tra 7,2 e 7,6. Il cloro aiuterà a distruggere i microrganismi, i funghi e i batteri e a mantenere l'acqua pulita.

Controla el pH del agua al menos una vez por semana. El valor del pH debe estar entre 7,2 y 7,6. El cloro ayudará a destruir microorganismos, hongos y bacterias, y a mantener el agua limpia.

Out of the blue, Mira Marinazzo

Faulkner & Chapman Landscape Design
Brighton, Australia
(left)

Mallorca, Spain
(right)

Mallorca, Spain
(opposite page)

Do not throw chlorine tablets into the pool because it might burn the paint on the bottom and leave white stains. If the water has a green hue, regulate the pH with a pH increaser or reducer. Remove dead algae, because they are the cause of the problem.

Gooi chloortabletten nooit rechtstreeks in het zwembad. Ze kunnen de verf op de bodem verbranden en witte vlekken veroorzaken. Als het water groenig is, regel de pH dan met een ph-verhoger of verlager. Zuig dode algen weg, omdat die de oorzaak van het probleem zijn.

Werfen Sie keine Chlortabletten direkt in den Swimmingpool, da sie die Farbe am Boden zerstören können und weiße Flecken hinterlassen. Wenn das Wasser grünlich wird, regulieren Sie den pH-Wert mit einem pH-Verstärker oder Reduktionsmittel. Saugen Sie die toten Algen ab, denn sie sind die Verursacher des Problems.

Non gettate pastiglie di cloro direttamente in piscina, perché potrebbero bruciare la pittura sul fondo e lasciare macchie bianche. Se l'acqua assume una colorazione verde regolate l'acidità con un accrescitore o riduttore di pH. Aspirate le alghe morte, che sono la causa del problema.

Ne jetez pas de pastilles de chlore directement dans la piscine, ces dernières peuvent en effet brûler la peinture du fond et faire apparaître des tâches blanches. Si l'eau présente une tonalité verte, régulez le pH à l'aide d'un rehausseur ou réducteur de pH. Aspirez les algues mortes à l'origine du problème.

No tires pastillas de cloro directamente a la piscina porque podría quemar la pintura del fondo y dejar manchas blancas. Si el agua presenta una tonalidad verde, regula el pH con un incrementador o reductor de pH. Succiona las algas muertas, porque son las causantes del problema.

Santorini, Greece

Mollégés, France
(opposite page)

Mallorca, Spain

Santorini, Greece
(left)

Out of the blue, Mira Marinazzo
(right)

In small gardens, the chromatic range of the flowers should be simple. One idea is to choose two or three basic colors.

In kleine tuinen moet het kleurengamma van de bloemen eenvoudig zijn. Een idee is om te kiezen voor twee of drie basiskleuren.

Kleine Gärten sollten nicht zu bunt sein. Eine Möglichkeit ist es, zwei oder drei Grundfarben zu wählen.

Nei piccoli giardini, la gamma cromatica dei fiori dovrebbe essere semplice. Sarebbe bene scegliere soltanto due o tre colori primari.

Dans les petits jardins, la gamme chromatique des fleurs doit être simple. Une idée consiste à opter pour deux ou trois couleurs de base.

En los jardines pequeños, la gama cromática de las flores debería ser sencilla. Una idea es optar por dos o tres colores básicos.

CCS Architecture
Sonoma, CA, USA
(left)

Flowers at home should not be in the path of direct sunlight and should not be exposed to drafts or high temperatures. Vases must be very clean and when we put the flowers in we must cut those that are submerged.

Bloemen in huis mogen niet worden blootgesteld aan direct zonlicht, noch aan tocht of hoge temperaturen. De vazen moeten schoon zijn en als we de bloemen op de vaas zetten moeten we de bloemen die onder water komen afknippen.

Bei Blumen im Haus sollte man die direkte Sonneneinstrahlung vermeiden und sie weder Windzug noch hohen Temperaturen aussetzen. Die Vasen sollten sehr sauber sein. Wenn wir die Blumen hineinstellen, müssen wir diejenigen, die sich unter Wasser befinden, abschneiden.

I fiori all'interno della casa devono essere al riparo dall'irraggiamento diretto e non devono essere esposti alle correnti d'aria né a temperature troppo alte. Le fioriere devono essere molto pulite e quando collochiamo i fiori dobbiamo tagliare quelli che sono sovrastati dagli altri.

Les fleurs d'intérieur ne doivent pas être exposées de façon directe aux rayons du soleil, aux courants d'air ni aux températures élevées. Les vases doivent être très propres et les fleurs submergées lors de leur mise en place dans le récipient doivent être coupées.

En casa, evita exponer las flores a la luz directa del sol, a las corrientes de aire y a temperaturas altas. Los floreros deben estar muy limpios y cuando se coloquen las flores conviene cortar aquellas que queden sumergidas.

One way to have an endless supply of flowers is to grow both perennials and bulbs specimens suitable for cut flowers in the garden. Some examples are the carnation, chrysanthemum, the carnation, lilac or bulbs such as tulips, lilies or spikenard.

Eine Möglichkeit, immer Blumen im Haus zu haben, ist es, im Garten sowohl mehrjährige als auch immergrüne Arten als Schnittblumen anzupflanzen, wie z.B. Nelken, Chrysanthemen, Bartnelken, Flieder, Tulpen, Narden oder Lilien.

Pour avoir toujours des fleurs disponibles dans la maison, une solution consiste à cultiver dans le jardin les espèces capables de produire des fleurs coupées, qu'elles soient vivaces, persistantes ou bulbeuses. Tel est le cas des œillets, des chrysanthèmes, des petits œillets, du lilas ou des plantes à bulbes comme la tulipe, le nard ou le lis.

Een manier om altijd bloemen in huis te hebben is om zelf snijbloemen in de tuin te kweken, zowel soorten met altijd groene bladeren als bolgewassen. Voorbeelden zijn anjers, chrysanten, anjeliers, seringen, tulpeb, nardussen of lelies.

Un modo per avere sempre fiori disponibili per abbellire la casa è coltivare in giardino varietà di piante specifiche da fiore reciso, sia vivaci che perenni o bulbose. Alcuni esempi sono il garofano, il crisantemo, il garofano selvatico e il lillà, o bulbose come il tulipano, la tuberosa o il giglio.

Una forma de tener siempre flores disponibles en casa es cultivar en el jardín las especies aptas para flor cortada, tanto vivaces como perennes y bulbosas. Algunos ejemplos son el clavel, el crisantemo, la clavellina, la lila, el tulipán, el nardo o la azucena.

Buenos Aires, Argentina

Buenos Aires, Argentina
(this page)

Ornaments with fresh flowers allow you to change the decor every week or whenever you want to brighten up a space. The combination of seasonal flowers with bright colors enhances an aisle or window.

Door versieringen met verse bloemen kan de decoratie wekelijks worden veranderd, en altijd als we een ruimte willen opvrolijken. De combinatie van seizoensbloemen met levendige kleuren doen een gang of een raam beter uitkomen.

Mit frischem Blumenschmuck kann man die Wohnung jede Woche neu dekorieren und immer dann, wenn wir einen Raum freundlich gestalten möchten. Die Kombination von Blumen der Jahreszeit mit lebhaften Farben verschönert einen Flur ein Fenster.

L'utilizzo di fiori freschi come ornamento permette di cambiare questi elementi decorativi ogni settimana, oppure ogni volta che per un motivo qualsiasi ci proporremo di rallegrare un ambiente. Una composizione di fiori di stagione dai colori luminosi renderà più bello un corridoio o di finestra.

Les ornements de fleurs fraîches permettent de chan la décoration toutes les semaines ou à chaque fois que à égayer un espace. La combinaison de fleurs de saisor vives améliorera le caractère d'une allée ou d'une fenêt

Los ornamentos con flores frescas permiten cambiar la cada semana o siempre que queramos alegrar un espa combinación de flores de temporada con colores vivos el aspecto de un pasillo o una ventana.

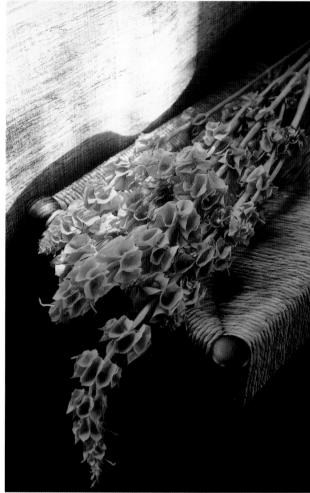

Indoor plants usually need plenty of light. However, there are species that survive perfectly with a low level of light. You should put plants requiring more light in rooms that face south. And in the north, those that require less intense light.

Kamerplanten hebben vaak veel licht nodig. Er zijn echter ook soorten die perfect gedijen in weinig licht. Zet planten die meer licht nodig hebben in kamers die op het zuiden liggen en planten die aan weinig licht voldoende hebben op het noorden.

Zimmerpflanzen brauchen in der Regel viel Licht. Es gibt jedoch Arten, die sehr gut mit wenig Licht auskommen. Pflanzen, die mehr Licht brauchen, stellen wir in Räumen auf, die nach Süden gehen, Pflanzen, die weniger intensives Licht benötigen, in Räumen, die nach Norden ausgerichtet sind.

In generale le piante da interno hanno bisogno di luce in abbondanza, anche se non mancano specie che vivono perfettamente con poca luce. Le piante che hanno bisogno di più luce dovranno essere collocate in stanze che danno sulla facciata sud. A nord, metteremo quelle che richiedono meno luminosità.

Les plantes d'intérieur ont généralement besoin de beaucoup de lumière. Certaines espèces n'en requièrent toutefois que très peu. Les plantes gourmandes en lumière doivent être placées dans des chambres exposées plein sud. Les autres doivent quant à elles être placées dans les chambres orientées vers le nord.

Las plantas de interior generalmente necesitan luz abundante. Sin embargo, hay especies que viven perfectamente con poca luz. Las plantas que necesiten más luz deberemos colocarlas en habitaciones orientadas al sur. En las estancias orientadas al norte, las que requieran menos intensidad luminosa.

To ensure that a cactus blooms, in winter keep the plant indoors in a bright spot. Give it minimal water and no fertilizer. Some species only flower if they withstand a coldstroke during the winter. The cactus flower is very attractive but short-lived

Damit Kakteen blühen, sollte man die Pflanzen im Winter innerhalb des Hauses an einem hellen Ort ruhen lassen. Geben sie sehr wenig Wasser und keinen Dünger. Manche Arten blühen nur, wenn sie im Winter einen Kälteschock erlitten haben. Eine Kaktusblüte ist sehr attraktiv, aber kurzlebig.

Pour garantir la floraison des cactus, il convient de rentrer la plante à l'intérieur de la maison en hiver en la plaçant dans un endroit lumineux. Arrosez-la d'un minimum d'eau et n'utilisez aucun engrais. Certaines espèces ne fleurissent que lorsqu'elles subissent un coup de froid pendant l'hiver. Bien qu'elle soit éphémère, la fleur de cactus est très attirante.

Om de bloei van een cactus te garanderen is het raadzaam om de plant in de winter binnen te laten rusten op een lichte plaats. Geef hem minimaal water en helemaal geen mest. Sommige soorten bloeien alleen als ze gedurende de winter kortstondig aan de kou zijn blootgesteld. De bloem van de cactus is prachtig, maar van korte duur.

Per garantire la fioritura dei cactus conviene lasciare la pianta a riposo durante l'inverno dentro la casa in un ambiente luminoso. Fornisci loro una quantità d'acqua minima evitando di concimarli. Alcune specie fioriscono solo se durante l'inverno soffrono un periodo freddo. Il fiore del cactus è molto spettacolare anche se effimero.

Para garantizar la floración de los cactus es conveniente dejarlos reposar durante el invierno dentro de casa y en un sitio luminoso. Requieren el mínimo de agua y nada de abono. Algunas especies solo florecen si soportan un golpe de frío durante el invierno. La flor del cactus es de un gran atractivo aunque es efímera.

Ecogarden: climate control, green roofs and walls

Ökologischer Garten: Klimakontrolle, begrünte
Dächer und Wände

Éco-jardin : contrôle climatique, toits
et murs verts

Eco-tuin: luchtbehandeling, groene daken
en muren

Eco-giardino: controllo climatico, tetti
e muri verdi

Ecojardín: control climático, cubiertas
y paredes vegetales

Having a sustainable organic garden is not difficult if your habits and attitude contribute to environmental protection and conservation.

The main challenges to avoid a bad crop are: saving water, pesticides and fertilizers. If there is little water for irrigation it is recommended to plant cacti and other succulents. You can use organic fertilizers such as vermicompost, manure, mulch, compost or peat moss.

When choosing plants select those that suit the climate and soil of the garden. Each climate has its appropriate vegetation and each garden has its microclimates. Light, temperature, rainfall, humidity and winds are climatic-environmental factors that influence the choice of plants. It is also important to know the terrain. The texture, depth, drainage, pH, mineral nutrients of the land not only influence the choice of species, but also the irrigation systems. The most appropriate system is one that has a flow and water pressure regulator as well as a timer indicating the beginning and end of irrigation. Another advanced irrigation system is underground irrigation. Perforated pipes are buried in the ground replacing conventional sprinklers and nozzles. And finally, another system for those plants that do not receive water from watering the lawn, for example, drip or localized irrigation.

Climbing plants, vines or climbing shrubs are a group of very interesting and useful plants, if you want to create a pleasant shade. They are also ideal for hiding a wall, softening corners and creating green galleries in access points. Trees are also a good option to create shaded areas in the garden. Lindens, for example, are very effective as a sunshade. During the winter the bare branches do not affect the light and in the summer they cool down the space thanks to the shade that the leaves create.

Avoir un jardin écologique et durable n'est pas difficile ; il suffit d'encourager les pratiques et habitudes qui contribuent à la préservation de l'environnement.

Les principaux défis pour éviter une mauvaise culture sont : l'économie d'eau, de produits phytosanitaires et d'engrais. Si vous disposez de peu d'eau pour l'arrosage, il est recommandé de planter des cactus et autres plantes grasses. Il est possible de n'utiliser que des engrais organiques, comme de l'humus de vers de terre, du fumier, du terreau, du compost ou de la tourbe.

Au moment de choisir ses plantes, il faut sélectionner celles qui s'adaptent le mieux au climat et au sol du jardin. Chaque climat a sa végétation appropriée et chaque jardin possède ses propres microclimats. La lumière, les températures, la pluie, l'humidité et les vents sont des facteurs climatiques et environnementaux qui auront une influence sur le choix des plantes. Il est également important de connaître le sol. La texture, la profondeur, le drainage, le pH ou les nutriments minéraux du terrain auront non seulement une influence sur le choix des espèces, mais également sur celui des systèmes d'arrosage. Le système le plus approprié est celui qui dispose d'un régulateur de débit et de pression de l'eau, ainsi qu'une minuterie indiquant le début et la fin de l'arrosage. Un autre système d'arrosage avancé est l'arrosage souterrain. Il s'agit de tuyaux perforés, enterrés dans le sol, qui remplacent les asperseurs et diffuseurs classiques. Enfin, un autre système adapté aux plantes qui ne reçoivent pas d'eau de l'arrosage de la pelouse, par exemple, est le goutte-à-goutte ou l'arrosage localisé.

Les plantes grimpantes ou les arbustes grimpants sont un groupe de plantes très intéressant et utile si l'on souhaite créer une ombre agréable. Ces plantes sont également idéales pour dissimuler un mur, adoucir des angles ou former des galeries vertes sur les chemins d'accès. Les arbres sont également une bonne option pour créer des zones d'ombre dans le jardin. Les tilleuls, par exemple, font parfaitement office de parasols. Pendant l'hiver, les branches dépouillées bloquent à peine le passage de la lumière, et en été, elles tempèrent l'espace grâce à la zone d'ombre créée par leurs feuilles.

Einen ökologischen, nachhaltigen Garten zu haben ist nicht schwer, wenn man Gewohnheiten und Verhalten pflegt, die zum Erhalt und zum Schutz der Umwelt beitragen.

Die wichtigsten Prinzipien zur Vermeidung einer schlechten Bepflanzung sind: sparsame Verwendung von Wasserer, Pflanzenschutzmitteln und Düngemitteln. Wenn man wenig Wasser zum Gießen hat, empfehlen wir, Kakteen und andere Sukkulenten anzupflanzen. Wenn möglich sollte man nur mit Düngemitteln auf organischer Basis, wie Wurmhumus, Mist, Mulch, Kompost oder Torf düngen.

Wenn man die Pflanzen aussucht, sollte man diejenigen wählen, die an das Klima und den Boden des Gartens angepasst sind. Jedes Klima hat seine entsprechende Vegetation und jeder Garten hat sein eigenes Mikroklima. Licht, Temperatur, Regen und Wind sind Klima- und Umweltfaktoren, die die Auswahl der Pflanzen beeinflussen. Es ist auch wichtig, den Boden zu kennen. Konsistenz, Tiefe, Entwässerung, pH-Wert oder mineralische Nährstoffe des Geländes haben nicht nur Einfluss auf die Auswahl der Arten, sondern auch auf die Bewässerungssysteme. Am geeignetsten ist ein System, das mit einem Wasser-Durchfluss- und Druckregler ausgestattet ist, sowie mit einer Zeitschaltuhr, die Beginn und Ende der Bewässerung angibt. Ein weiteres fortschrittliches Bewässerungssystem ist die unterirdische Bewässerung. Es handelt sich um perforierte Schlauchleitungen, die in den Boden eingelassen sind und die klassischen Rasensprenger ersetzen. Und schließlich gibt es noch ein weiteres System für die Pflanzen, die nicht vom Wasser des Rasensprengers erreicht werden, z.B. die Tröpfchen- oder Tropfbewässerung.

Kletterpflanzen, Schlingpflanzen oder Rankengewächse bilden eine sehr interessante und nützliche Pflanzengruppe, mit der man einen angenehmen Schatten schaffen kann. Sie sind auch ideal, um Mauern zu verstecken, Ecken abzurunden oder grüne Galerien über den Zugangswegen zu errichten. Auch Bäume sind eine gute Möglichkeit, um Schattenbereiche im Garten zu schaffen. Linden eignen sich z.B. sehr gut als Sonnenschirm. Im Winter nehmen die kahlen Äste kaum Licht weg und im Sommer bringen sie dank des Schattens, den ihre Blätter spenden, Kühlung.

Het houden van een ecologische en duurzame tuin is niet moeilijk als we er gewoontes en houdingen op nahouden die bijdragen aan het behoud en de bescherming van het milieu.

De belangrijkste uitdagingen voor goed tuinieren zijn: besparing van water, bestrijdingsmiddelen en kunstmest. Als er weinig water voorhanden is om te sproeien, dan is het raadzaam om te kiezen voor cactussen en andere vetplanten. Bemesten met alleen organische mest, zoals wormenhumus, mest, teelgrond, compost of turf is mogelijk.

Kies voor planten die zich aanpassen aan het klimaat en de grond van de tuin. Ieder klimaat heeft zijn eigen geschikte vegetatie en iedere tuin heeft zijn eigen microklimaten. Licht, temperatuur, regenval, vochtigheid en wind zijn klimaat- en omgevingsfactoren die bepalend zijn voor de keuze voor de planten. Ook is het belangrijk om de eigenschappen van de grond te kennen. Textuur, diepte, drainage, pH of minerale voedingsstoffen van het terrein zijn niet alleen belangrijk bij deze keuze van planten, maar ook voor de besproeiingssystemen. Een geschikt systeem is voorzien van een debietregelaar en drukregelaar, alsmede een timer die het begin en einde van de besproeiing aangeeft. Een ander geavanceerd bevloeiingssyteem is ondergrondse irrigatie. Dit bestaat uit geperforeerde buizen die in de grond zijn ingegraven en klassieke sproeiers vervangen. Tenslotte is er een ander systeem voor planten waar de gazonsproeiers niet komen, namelijk druppelbevloeiing.

Klimplanten, slingerplanten of klimheesters vormen een interessante en nuttige plantengroep om een aangename schaduw te scheppen. Ze zijn ook ideaal om een muur achter te verbergen, scherpe hoeken af te zwakken of om groene galerijen langs opritten te maken. Ook bomen zijn een goede optie om schaduwzones in de tuin te verkrijgen. Lindes doen bijvoorbeeld goed dienst als parasol. In de winter nemen de naakte takken nauwelijks licht weg, terwijl ze in de zomer de warmte matigen dankzij het schaduwscherm dat door de bladeren ontstaat.

Avere un giardino ecologico e sostenibile non è difficile se si fomentano consuetudini e atteggiamenti che contribuiscono alla conservazione ed alla protezione dell'ambiente.

Le principali sfide per evitare una cattiva coltivazione sono: il risparmio dell'acqua, di prodotti fitosanitari e di concimi. Qualora si disponga di poca acqua per innaffiare, si raccomanda di piantare cactus ed altre piante grasse. Si può concimare limitandosi all'uso di concimi organici, come humus di lombrico, sterco, terricciato, compost o torba.

Quando si scelgono le piante bisogna selezionare quelle adatte sia al clima che alla terra del giardino. Ogni clima ha una vegetazione appropriata ed ogni giardino possiede i propri microclimi. La luce, le temperature, la pioggia, l'umidità ed i venti sono fattori climatico-ambientali che influiranno sulla scelta delle piante. È importante, inoltre, conoscere il terreno. La tessitura, la profondità, il drenaggio, il pH o i nutrienti minerali della terra non solo influenzeranno la scelta delle specie ma anche quella dei sistemi d'irrigazione. Il sistema più adatto è quello che dispone di un regolatore di portata e della pressione dell'acqua, nonché di un temporizzatore che indichi l'inizio e la fine dell'irrigazione. Un altro sistema d'irrigazione avanzato è costituito dall'irrigazione interrata. Si tratta di tubature perforate interrate che sostituiscono i classici irrigatori e diffusori, ed infine, un altro sistema per le piante alle quali non arriva l'acqua dell'irrigazione del prato verde è, ad esempio, l'irrigazione a goccia o localizzata.

Le piante murali e rampicanti o gli arbusti rampicanti sono piante molto interessanti ed utili per creare piacevoli zone d'ombra. Sono, infatti, ideali per occultare muri, addolcire angoli o formare gallerie verdi nei sentieri d'accesso. Gli alberi costituiscono un'altra buona opzione per creare zone d'ombra nel giardino. I tigli, ad esempio, sono dei parasoli ideali. Durante l'inverno, i rami spogli danno passo alla luce del sole, mentre durante l'estate rinfrescano gli spazi grazie all'ombra creata dalla loro rigogliosa chioma verde.

Tener un jardín ecológico y sostenible no es difícil si se fomentan hábitos y actitudes que contribuyan a la conservación y protección del medioambiente.

Los principales retos para evitar un mal cultivo son: el ahorro de agua, de productos fitosanitarios y de abonos. Si se dispone de poca agua para regar se recomienda plantar cactus y otras crasas. Se puede abonar sólo a base de abonos orgánicos, como humus de lombriz, estiércol, mantillo, compost o turba.

Cuando se escogen las plantas hay que seleccionar aquellas que se adapten al clima y al suelo del jardín. Cada clima tiene su vegetación apropiada y cada jardín posee sus microclimas. La luz, las temperaturas, la lluvia, la humedad y los vientos son factores climático-ambientales que influirán en la elección de las plantas. También es importante conocer el suelo. De la textura, la profundidad, el drenaje, el pH o los nutrientes minerales del terreno dependerá no sólo la elección de las especies sino también los sistemas de riego. El sistema más apropiado es aquel que cuenta con un regulador de caudal y presión del agua, así como con un temporizador que indique el inicio y el final del riego. Otro sistema de riego avanzado es el riego subterráneo. Se trata de tuberías perforadas enterradas en el suelo que sustituyen los aspersores y difusores clásicos. Y finalmente, otro sistema para aquellas plantas que no les llega el agua del riego del césped, por ejemplo, es el riego por goteo o localizado.

Las plantas trepadoras, enredaderas o arbustos trepadores son un grupo de especies muy interesante y útil, si lo que se quiere es crear una agradable sombra. También son ideales para esconder un muro, suavizar esquinas o formar galerías verdes en los caminos de acceso. También los árboles son una buena opción para crear zonas de sombra en el jardín. Los tilos, por ejemplo, actúan muy bien como sombrilla. Durante el invierno, las ramas desnudas apenas quitan luz, y en verano atemperan el espacio gracias a la pantalla de sombra que crean sus hojas.

To save water you can place a group of plants under the shade of a tree or a pergola with climbing plants to protect them from the sun.

Om water te besparen kan men een groep planten onder de schaduw van een boom of een pergola met klimop zetten, zodat ze beschermd worden tegen de zon.

Um Wasser zu sparen, kann man Pflanzen in Gruppen in den Schatten eines Baumes oder einer Pergola mit Kletterpflanzen setzen, damit sie vor der Sonne geschützt sind.

Per risparmiare acqua si può collocare un gruppo di piante all'ombra di un albero o di una pergola, con rampicanti che lo riparino dal sole.

Pour économiser l'eau, il est possible de placer un groupe de plantes à l'ombre d'un arbre ou d'une pergola agrémentée de plantes grimpantes afin de les protéger du soleil.

Para ahorrar agua se puede colocar un grupo de plantas bajo la sombra de un árbol o de una pérgola con trepadoras para que estén resguardadas del sol.

Arborètum
Barcelona, Spain

If you have olive trees in your terrace, enjoy their rural character. The olive tree is perhaps one of the most representative trees of the Mediterranean climate. Younger species that can be bought at specialist nurseries look very good on a balcony.

Mit Olivenbäumen auf der Terrasse kann man ein ländliches Ambiente schaffen. Der Olivenbaum ist einer der typischsten Vertreter des mediterranen Klimas. Auf einem Balkon machen sich junge Exemplare gut, die man in spezialisierten Gärtnereien kaufen kann.

Les propriétaires possédant des oliviers plantés en terrasse pourront profiter de leur esprit champêtre. L'olivier est probablement l'un des arbres les plus représentatifs du climat méditerranéen. Les jeunes spécimens, disponibles dans des pépinières spécialisées, font très bonne impression sur un balcon.

Eigenaren die olijven op het terras hebben staan, kunnen genieten van een landelijke sfeer. De olijfboom is misschien wel een van de meest kenmerkende bomen van het Middellandse Zeeklimaat. Op een balkon doen jonge exemplaren het goed. Ze zijn verkrijgbaar bij gespecialiseerde kwekerijen.

I proprietari di una casa che ha ulivi su una terrazza potranno sfruttare l'atmosfera bucolica che queste piante ispirano. L'ulivo è forse uno degli alberi più rappresentativi del clima mediterraneo. Su un balcone stanno molto bene gli esemplari giovani che possono essere comprati nei vivai specializzati.

Los propietarios que dispongan de olivos en la terraza podrán disfrutar de un ambiente rural. El olivo es quizás uno de los árboles más representativos del clima mediterráneo. En un balcón quedan muy bien los ejemplares jóvenes que se pueden comprar en viveros especializados.

Arborètum
Barcelona, Spain

When choosing species, remember that the color of the foliage is also very important. Aromatic plants are easily looked after and they maintain their shape with light pruning. Lavender is a good option and when in bloom it brings serenity to the garden with its color and aroma.

Bij het uitkiezen van een soort is de kleur van het gebladerte ook heel belangrijk. Aromatische plant geven ook uitstekende resultaten omdat die niet veel zorg nodig hebben en met weinig snoeien hun vorm behouden. Lavendel is een goede optie. De kleur en geur van bloeiende lavendel zorgen voor een tuin die rust uitstraalt.

Wenn Sie die Arten auswählen, müssen Sie beachten, dass die Farbe des Blattwerks auch sehr wichtig ist. Jede Art von Duftpflanze ist sehr dankbar, weil sie nicht viel Pflege braucht und man ihre Form durch leichtes Beschneiden bewahren kann. Lavendel ist eine gute Wahl, und wenn er blüht, bringt er mit seiner Farbe und seinem Duft Heiterkeit in den Garten.

Quando scegliete le diverse specie, tenete presente che il colore del fogliame è a sua volta molto importante. Qualsiasi aromatica è molto consigliata perché non richiede molte cure e se ne può mantenere la forma con leggere potature. La lavanda è una buona opzione e quando fiorisce dona un senso di serenità al giardino con il suo colore e il suo aroma.

À l'heure de choisir les espèces, tenir compte du fait que la couleur du feuillage est aussi très importante. N'importe quelle plante aromatique sera très appréciée. Ces espèces ne requièrent en effet que très peu de soins et peuvent conserver leur forme au moyen de tailles légères. La lavande est un excellent choix et sa floraison confère une certaine sérénité au jardin grâce à sa couleur et son arôme.

Cuando escojas las especies, ten en cuenta que el color del follaje también es muy importante. Cualquier aromática es muy agradecida porque no requiere muchos cuidados y puedes mantener su forma con ligeras podas. La lavanda es una buena opción y cuando florece aporta serenidad al jardín con su color y aroma.

Arborètum
Barcelona, Spain

Arborètum
Barcelona, Spain

A corner on the terrace, next to a fence and under a wooden pergola or cane screen provides shelter from the sun, and is he ideal location for spring dining. Wooden pergolas with vines, for example, can provide pleasant areas of sun and shade to the terrace.

Een hoekje op het terras, naast een hek en onder een houten en pergola met vlechtwerk van riet die de zon tegenhoudt is de ideale plaats voor een zomerse eethoek. Houten pergola's met bijvoorbeeld wingerdranken kunnen een aangenaam zon- en schaduwplekje op het terras creëren.

Eine Ecke auf der Terrasse, an einer Hecke oder unter einer Pergola aus Holz und Rohrgeflecht, die vor der Sonne schützt, ist der ideale Ort für einen frühlingshaften Essplatz. Weinumrankte Pergolas aus Holz, können eine angenehme Sonnen-und Schattenzone auf der Terrasse schaffen.

Un angolo della terrazza, vicino a una siepe o sotto una pergola di legno e canniccio che lo protegga dal sole, è l'ubicazione ideale per un tavolo da pranzo per la bella stagione. Le pergole di legno sulle quali si arrampica una vite rampicante, per esempio, possono donarci uno spazio in cui goderci l'ombra e il sole in questa zona della terrazza.

Un recoin de la terrasse, situé à côté d'une haie et sous une pergola en bois et une claie le protégeant du soleil, est l'emplacement idéal pour une zone de repas printanière. Les pergolas en bois agrémentées d'une vigne grimpante, par exemple, peuvent créer d'agréables espaces ensoleillés et ombragés sur la terrasse.

Un rincón en la terraza, junto a un seto y bajo una pérgola de madera y cañizo que lo proteja del sol, es la ubicación ideal para un comedor primaveral. Las pérgolas de madera por las que trepa una parra, por ejemplo, pueden crear una agradable zona de sol y sombra en la terraza.

If you want to achieve a rural feeling, randomly combine culinary and medicinal herbs with ornamental plants. Some aromatic herbs protect against pests so mixing them with other crops is a good way to control pests.

Als u een landelijke sfeer wilt creëren, combineer dan kruiden en medicinale planten met sierplanten, door ze schijnbaar willekeurig te combineren. Sommige aromatische kruiden werken als bescherming tegen plagen. Daarom is het raadzaam om ze met andere gewassen te combineren, om parasieten tegen te gaan.

Wenn Sie einen ländlichen Stil erreichen wollen, kombinieren Sie Gewürzkräuter und Heilpflanzen mit Zierpflanzen in einer scheinbar zufälligen Mischung. Manche Gewürzkräuter schützen gegen Schädlingsbefall; deshalb ist es ratsam, sie mit anderen Pflanzungen zu mischen, um die Parasiten unter Kontrolle zu halten.

Se volete ottenere uno stile campestre combinate erbe aromatiche e officinali con piante ornamentali, tutte mescolate tra loro. Alcune tra le erbe aromatiche hanno una funzione protettiva contro le malattie e per questo si raccomanda di mescolarle alle altre coltivazioni, così da tenere sotto controllo i parassiti.

Si vous souhaitez obtenir un style champêtre, combinez de manière en apparence aléatoire des herbes condimentaires et médicinales avec des plantes ornementales. Certaines herbes aromatiques jouent le rôle de protection contre les maladies. Il est donc recommandé de les mélanger aux autres cultures pour contrôler les parasites.

Si quieres conseguir un estilo campestre combina hierbas condimentarias y medicinales con plantas ornamentales, todas mezcladas aparentemente al azar. Algunas de las hierbas aromáticas actúan como protección contra las plagas, por eso es recomendable mezclarlas con otros cultivos para controlar los parásitos.

Arborètum
Barcelona, Spain

A shower in the garden can be a pleasant alternative to survive hot days. Teak deck chairs are a type of functional furnishing because teak is highly resistant to oxidation. To care for the wood, use special oil for teak and neutral soap.

Eine Dusche im Garten bietet eine angenehme Alternative während der heißen Tage. Teakholzliegen sind funktionelle Möbelstücke, da es sich um ein sehr wetterbeständiges Material handelt. Man pflegt es mit einem Spezialöl für Teakholz und neutraler Seife.

L'installation d'une douche dans un jardin peut représenter une solution agréable pour supporter les journées de chaleur. Les transats en bois de teck sont un type de mobilier fonctionnel puisque ce matériau résiste particulièrement bien à l'oxydation. Pour l'entretenir, il suffit d'y appliquer de l'huile spéciale pour bois de teck et du savon neutre.

Een douche in de tuin kan een aangenaam alternatief zijn voor verkoeling op warme dagen. Een teakhouten ligstoel is een functioneel meubelstuk, omdat het materiaal goed bestand is tegen roest. Het onderhoud bestaat uit het aanbrengen van speciale olie voor teakhout en neutrale zeep.

Una doccia in giardino può essere una piacevole alternativa per combattere i giorni di solleone. Le sdraio di legno di tek sono ottimi elementi per l'arredamento visto che questo materiale ha una buona resistenza all'ossidazione. La sua manutenzione consiste nell'applicare un olio speciale per tek e sapone neutro.

Una ducha en el jardín puede ser una agradable alternativa para combatir los días calurosos. Las tumbonas de madera de teca son un tipo de mobiliario funcional, ya que es un material con buena resistencia a la oxidación. Su cuidado consiste en aplicar aceite especial para teca y jabón neutro.

Arborètum
Barcelona, Spain

In warm climates, shade is a man's best friend. It does not only offer a break from direct sunlight for people, animals and plants, but it also has another important role, as it filters the air, water and noise.

In warme klimaten kan schaduw veranderen in de beste bondgenoot. Het biedt niet alleen bescherming tegen de zon voor mensen, dieren en planten, maar speelt nog een andere belangrijke rol, aangezien het lucht, water en geluid filtert.

Bei heißem Wetter wird der Schatten zum besten Freund. Er bietet nicht nur einen sonnengeschützten Ort für Menschen, Tiere und Pflanzen, sondern spielt noch eine weitere wichtige Rolle, da er die Luft, das Wasser und den Lärm filtert.

Nei climi caldi, l'ombra può diventare il nostro miglior alleato. Non solo offre un luogo fresco per riposare a persone, animali e vegetali, ma ha anche un altro ruolo essenziale: filtra l'aria, l'acqua e il rumore.

Dans les climats chauds, l'ombre peut devenir notre meilleur allié. Elle offre non seulement un lieu de repos à l'abri du soleil pour les personnes, les animaux et les végétaux, mais joue également un rôle important en filtrant l'air, l'eau et le bruit.

En climas cálidos, la sombra puede convertirse en el mejor aliado. Una sombrilla, un toldo o una cubierta no solo ofrecen un refugio del sol para personas, animales y plantas, sino que también tienen otro papel importante, pues filtran el aire, el agua y el ruido.

Ibiza, Spain

191

Ibiza, Spain
(this page)

Mario Connío
Mexico
(left)

Pergolas come in several shapes. They are never completely closed to have increased contact with nature. Green roofs will lend a beautiful style to the pergola, although you can use other natural materials such as cane.

Structuren van een pergola kunnen verschillende vormen hebben, maar mogen nooit helemaal afgesloten zijn, om een beter contact met de natuur te bieden. Groene daken geven de pergola een fraaie stijl, hoewel er ook andere natuurlijke materialen kunnen worden gebruikt, zoals vlechtwerk van riet.

Pergolas können verschiedene Formen haben, aber sie dürfen niemals vollkommen geschlossen sein, damit sie eine bessere Verbindung mit der Natur bieten. Pflanzendächer verleihen den Pergolas ein schönes Aussehen, aber man kann auch andere Naturmaterialien wie Rohrgeflecht verwenden.

Le strutture delle pergole possono essere di forme diverse ma non sono mai completamente chiuse per mantenere un maggior contatto con la natura. Il tetto vegetale donerà un bellissimo tocco di stile alla pergola, anche se si possono utilizzare altri materiali naturali come il canniccio.

Les structures des pergolas peuvent être de différentes formes mais ne sont jamais complètement fermées pour conserver un plus grand contact avec la nature. Les toits végétaux donneront un superbe style à la pergola, même s'il est possible d'utiliser d'autres matériaux naturels comme le roseau.

Las estructuras de las pérgolas pueden tener diversas formas pero nunca deben ser completamente cerradas para ofrecer un mayor contacto con la naturaleza. Los techos vegetales darán un hermoso estilo a la pérgola, aunque se pueden utilizar otros materiales naturales como el cañizo.

Ibiza, Spain
(this page)

Plants and vines growing around the porch should be adapted to the climate and soil, factors such as temperature, light, wind, water, soil texture and rich nutrients will all influence. Do not allow it to grow excessively, prune it adequately. Make sure that the leaves and roots do not block drains or clearance holes.

Pflanzen und Schlingpflanzen, die um die Veranda herum wachsen, müssen an das Klima und an den für sie bestimmten Boden angepasst sein. Faktoren wie Temperatur, Licht, Wind, Wasser, Konsistenz des Bodens und Nährstoffreichtum spielen eine entscheidende Rolle. Lassen Sie nicht zu, dass sie zu üppig wachsen, und beschneiden Sie sie entsprechend. Passen Sie auf, dass keine Blätter und Wurzeln Abflüsse oder Durchgänge verstopfen.

Les plantes et les espèces grimpantes qui poussent autour du porche doivent être adaptées au climat et au sol qui leur est réservé. Les facteurs comme la température, la lumière, le vent, l'eau, la texture du sol et la richesse en nutriments auront une influence. Ne les laissez pas pousser de façon démesurée, taillez-les correctement. Veillez à ce que les feuilles et les racines n'obstruent pas des orifices d'écoulement ou de passage.

Planten en klimplanten die rond de galerij groeien, moeten zich kunnen aanpassen aan het klimaat en de grond waar ze geplaatst worden. Factoren als temperatuur, licht, wind, water, textuur van de grond en rijkheid van de voedingsstoffen zijn daarop van invloed. Voorkom dat ze gaan woekeren en snoei ze daarom goed. Zorg ervoor dat de bladeren en de wortels geen afvoeren of andere openingen bedekken.

Le piante e i rampicanti che crescono intorno al portico devono essere adatti al clima e al terreno che si è riservato per loro. Incideranno fattori quali la temperatura, la luce, il vento, l'acqua, la composizione del suolo e la ricchezza di sostanze nutritive. Non permettete che crescano in modo esagerato, potatele adeguatamente. Vigilate inoltre sul fatto che foglie e radici non ostruiscano canalette o bocchette di scolo.

Las plantas y las enredaderas que crezcan alrededor del porche deben adaptarse al clima y al suelo que les tengas reservado. Incidirán factores como la temperatura, la luz, el viento, el agua, la textura del suelo y la riqueza de nutrientes. No permitas su crecimiento desmesurado, pódalas adecuadamente. Ten la precaución de vigilar que las hojas y las raíces no tapen desagües o agujeros de paso.

Ibiza, Spain

The power of nature is reflected in these exteriors that have partly covered porches and pergolas, under which the outdoors dining areas are located where the vegetation and the setting are the most important elements.

De kracht van de natuur komt hier tot uiting met halfoverdekte veranda`s en pergola's, waaronder eethoeken zijn ingericht waar de vegetatie en de omgeving de belangrijkste elementen zijn.

Die Kraft der Natur zeigt sich in diesen Außenräumen mit Veranden und halb überdachten Pergolas, unter denen sich Essplätze im Freien befinden, wo die Vegetation und die Umwelt am wichtigsten sind.

La forza della natura si riflette in questi esterni che si costituiscono attraverso portici e pergolati semicoperti; al di sotto si trovano tavoli da pranzo in esterno rispetto ai quali la vegetazione e l'ambiente circostante sono gli elementi più importanti.

Le pouvoir de la nature se reflète dans ces espaces extérieurs aménagés de porches et de pergolas partiellement couverts, sous lesquels sont installées des zones repas extérieures où la végétation et les alentours constituent les éléments phares.

La fuerza de la naturaleza se refleja en estos exteriores que cuentan con porches y pérgolas semicubiertos, bajo los cuales se encuentran comedores exteriores donde la vegetación y el entorno son los elementos más importantes.

Daniel Zimmermann / 3:0 Landschaftsarchitektur
Vienna, Austria

Bart Haverkamp & Pieter Croes / Groendesigners
Amberes, Belgium
(opposite page)

New York, NY, USA
(this page)

To reduce noise contamination, pollution and other particles that the surrounding streets may cause, opt for a green expanse in addition to providing oxygen, it will create a cooler and private atmosphere.

Ter bescherming tegen de geluidshinder die veroorzaakt wordt door de omringende straten, de vervuiling en overige deeltjes, kan men kiezen voor een plantaardig scherm dat bovendien zuurstof geeft, verfrist en zorgt voor privacy.

Daniel Zimmermann / 3:0 Landschaftsarchitektur
Vienna, Austria

Studiebureau Groenplanning bvba
Amberes, Belgium
(opposite page)

Um die Lärmbelästigung durch die umgebenden Straßen, die Luftverschmutzung und andere Partikel zu reduzieren, kann man sich für eine Abschirmung durch Pflanzen entscheiden, die außer Sauerstoff noch Erfrischung und Privatsphäre bieten.

Per ridurre l'inquinamento acustico e atmosferico provocato dalle strade circostanti si può optare per una schermatura vegetale che, oltre a produrre ossigeno, raffrescherà e donerà intimità.

Pour réduire les nuisances sonores générées par les rues environnantes, la pollution ambiante et toute autre particule, il est possible d'envisager la mise en œuvre d'un écran végétal qui, en plus de fournir de l'oxygène, rafraîchira l'espace et conférera intimité.

Para reducir la contaminación acústica y la polución que puedan provocar las calles circundantes, se puede optar por una pantalla vegetal que, además de aportar oxígeno, refrescará y dará intimidad.

The garden areas at various levels extend the living areas and create a green world around the house. On the top floor, a pergola and the combination of typical garden plants such as magnolias, Japanese maples, ornamental apple trees, climbing roses, boxwood and hostas defines the environment.

Als tuin ingerichte ruimtes op verschillende niveaus maken het woongedeelte groter en scheppen een groene wereld rond het huis. Op de bovenverdieping wordt de sfeer bepaald door een pergola en door de combinatie van typische tuinplanten zoals magnolia's, Japanse esdoorns, sierappelbomen, klimrozen, buksen en hosta's.

Grünzonen auf verschiedenen Ebenen vergrößern die Wohnräume und schaffen eine grüne Welt rund um das Haus. Im oberen Stockwerk wird die Umgebung durch eine Pergola und die Kombination von typischen Pflanzen wie Magnolien, japanischem Ahorn, Zierapfelbäumen, Kletterrosen, Buchsbaum und Funkien geprägt.

Gli spazi a giardino su diversi livelli ampliano la zona abitabile e creano un mondo verde intorno alla casa. Al piano superiore, personalizzano l'ambiente una pergola e una composizione di piante da giardino come magnolie, aceri giapponesi, meli ornamentali, rose rampicanti, bossi e hoste.

Les pièces aménagées en jardin aux différents étages agrandissent les zones habitables et créent un monde verdoyant autour de la maison. À l'étage supérieur, l'atmosphère est générée par une pergola et la combinaison de plantes typiques du jardin comme les magnolias, les érables japonais, les pommiers ornementaux, les rosiers grimpants, les buis et les hostas.

Las estancias ajardinadas en los distintos niveles amplían las zonas habitables y crean un mundo verde alrededor de la casa. La planta superior queda definida por una pérgola y la combinación de plantas típicas de jardín como magnolias, arces japoneses, manzanos ornamentales, rosales trepadores, bojes y hostas.

New York, NY, USA

New York, NY, USA

n the roof of the building, a graphic composition in areas of
ravel and succulent plants acts as a liaison between the various
arts of the garden.

o het dak van een gebouw doet een grafische compositie in de
rindzones dienst als verbindingselement tussen de verschillende
elen van de tuin.

Auf dem Dach des Gebäudes dient eine grafische Komposition aus
Kies und Sukkulenten als Verbindung zwischen den verschiedenen
Abschnitten des Gartens.

Sulla copertura dell'edificio, una composizione a puzzle con linee
di ghiaia e succulente collega tra loro le varie parti del giardino.

Sur le toit du bâtiment, une composition graphique de zones
gravillonnées et de crassulacées joue le rôle de lien entre
les différentes parties du jardin.

En la cubierta del edificio, una composición gráfica en zonas de
gravilla y suculentas actúa de enlace entre las distintas partes
del jardín.

New York, NY, USA

Arborètum
Barcelona, Spain
(opposite page)

Birkenwerder, Germany

In addition to protection from the sun, green roofs have other properties. On the one hand, they aesthetically improve the building. On the other hand, the green roof improves the microclimate of the setting, because the roof surface becomes much cooler, the plants provide moisture and improve air quality by absorbing CO_2 and providing O_2.

Naast bescherming tegen de zon bieden begroeide daken nog andere voordelen. Enerzijds verbeteren ze het gebouw in esthetisch opzicht. Anderzijds verbeteren ze het microklimaat van de omgeving, doordat het oppervlak van het dak verandert in een koelere plaats. De planten leveren vocht en verbeteren de luchtkwaliteit, doordat ze kooldioxide opnemen en zuurstof afgeven.

Zusätzlich zum Schutz vor der Sonne haben begrünte Dächer weitere Vorteile. Zum einen verschönern sie das Gebäude durch einen lebendigen Raum. Zum anderen verbessern sie das Mikroklima der Umgebung, weil die Dachfläche zu einem viel frischeren Ort wird. Die Pflanzen bringen Feuchtigkeit und verbessern die Luftqualität, indem sie Kohlendioxid absorbieren und die Luft mit Sauerstoff anreichern.

Oltre a proteggere dall'irraggiamento solare, le coperture vegetalizzate hanno altre proprietà. In primo luogo migliorano esteticamente l'edificio; sul lungo periodo, inoltre, i tetti verdi migliorano il microclima del luogo, perché la superficie diventa uno spazio molto più fresco, le piante producono umidità e migliorano la capacità dell'aria di assorbire anidride carbonica e fornire ossigeno.

En plus de servir de protection solaire, les toitures végétales possèdent d'autres propriétés. D'une part, elles participent de l'esthétique du bâtiment. D'autre part, la toiture verte améliore le microclimat du milieu, car la surface du toit se convertit en un endroit beaucoup plus frais où les plantes apportent de l'humidité et bonifient la qualité de l'air en absorbant le CO_2 et en dégageant de l'O_2.

Además de la protección solar, las cubiertas vegetales tienen otras ventajas. Por un lado, mejoran estéticamente el edificio. Por otro lado, mejoran el microclima del entorno, porque la superficie del tejado se convierte en un lugar mucho más fresco, las plantas aportan humedad y mejoran la calidad del aire al absorber dióxido de carbono y proporcionar oxígeno.

Terraces, courtyards, balconies and indoor gardens

Terrassen, Innenhöfe und Wintergärten

Terrasses, cours, balcons et jardins intérieurs

Terrassen, binnenplaatsen, balkons en binnentuinen

Terrazzi, cortile, balconi e giardini interni

Terrazas, patios, balcones y jardines interiores

Terraces are ideal spaces to convert into a small garden, where not only do the selected species count but also the design of furniture and ornaments, which will add to its individual style.
Before planting, study the properties of the terrace, the environmental aspects to be able to adapt it to its environment and its real space. This will help transform it into a small, pretty, elegant garden. Terraces facing east foster the cultivation of almost everything as it only receives gentle sunlight and does not harm the plants. Conversely, if the roof faces north, opt for plants that require less light.
Courtyards are usually smaller areas where the sun does not shine so directly and therefore species that grow well in the shade or partial shade can flourish. If well designed they can be very intimate and cozy.
Balconies are usually wasted space, often with few square meters. However, they can become an extension of the interior and thus not only improve the view but become a comfortable vantage point with abundant vegetation.
Indoor gardens and courtyards are perhaps not as well known but certainly just as pleasant. Such spaces are converted in the lungs of the house because they are in the heart of the space and other rooms are distributed around them maximizing ventilation and natural light. Just like an exterior space, they can have grass, flowers and even trees that are adapted to the climate and terrain of the yard. They are suitable for those households who want to enjoy a vegetated area even in the interior, with access from a bedroom, bathroom or any other point.
Such interventions stand out not only for their ability to create a natural environment inside the home but also for the plants' properties to purify the air.

Les terrasses sont des espaces idéaux à transformer en petits jardins où les espèces choisies sont importantes, mais où le mobilier et la décoration comptent également pour définir un style personnel. Avant de commencer à cultiver les plantes, il faut étudier les propriétés de la terrasse et les aspects environnementaux, afin de pouvoir l'adapter à son espace réel, et l'arranger en un petit jardin agréable et élégant. Les terrasses orientées à l'est permettent de cultiver presque tout car le soleil qu'elles reçoivent est doux et ne nuit pas aux plantes. À l'inverse, si la terrasse est orientée au nord, il faudra choisir des plantes demandant moins de lumière.
Les cours sont généralement des zones plus restreintes dans lesquelles le soleil n'entre pas aussi directement ; elles sont donc adaptées à des espèces qui se développent bien dans l'ombre, totale ou partielle. Lorsqu'elles sont bien organisées, elles peuvent être très intimes et accueillantes.
Les balcons sont généralement des espaces peu utilisés, bien souvent petits. Cependant, en devenant la prolongation de l'espace intérieur, ils peuvent ainsi améliorer la vue, mais également disposer d'une devanture accueillante et d'une végétation abondante.
Moins connus, mais tout aussi agréables, sont les cours et jardins intérieurs. Ces espaces deviennent le cœur de la maison, car ils sont situés au centre, avec les autres pièces réparties autour, pour exploiter au maximum la ventilation et la lumière naturelle. Tout comme les espaces extérieurs, ils peuvent avoir de la pelouse, des fleurs et même des arbres, qui s'adaptent aux conditions climatiques et au terrain de la cour. Ces espaces sont adaptés pour les logements où l'on souhaite profiter d'un espace vert tout en restant à l'intérieur, accessible depuis une chambre, depuis une salle de bains ou depuis tout autre point.
Ce type d'espace se distingue non seulement par sa capacité à créer un environnement naturel à l'intérieur du logement, mais également par la faculté des plantes à purifier l'air.

Terrassen eignen sich hervorragend dazu, einen kleinen Garten zu gestalten, in dem nicht nur die gewählten Pflanzenarten, sondern auch das Design der Möbel und dekorativen Gegenstände, die ihm einen eigenen Stil verleihen, eine Rolle spielen. Bevor man mit der Bepflanzung beginnt, muss man die Eigenschaften der Terrasse und die Umweltaspekte untersuchen, damit man sie an ihre Umgebung und die gegebenen Räumlichkeiten anpassen kann. Auf diese Weise kann man die Terrasse in einen kleinen hübschen und eleganten Garten verwandeln. Auf Terrassen, die nach Osten gelegen sind, kann man fast alles pflanzen, da die einfallenden Sonnenstrahlen nicht zu stark sind und die Pflanzen nicht schädigen. Dagegen muss man für eine Terrasse, die nach Norden geht, Pflanzen wählen, die weniger Licht brauchen.
Innenhöfe sind normalerweise kleinere Bereiche, in die die Sonne nicht direkt hinein scheint. Deshalb sind sie für Pflanzen, die gern im Schatten oder Halbschatten wachsen, geeignet. Wenn man diese Innenhöfe gut plant, können sie sehr lauschig und gemütlich sein.
Balkone werden normalerweise nicht genutzt, in vielen Fällen sind sie nur wenige Quadratmeter groß. Sie können jedoch in eine Erweiterung des Innenraums verwandelt werden: so verbessern sie nicht nur die Aussicht, sondern werden auch zu einem einladenden Schaufenster mit üppiger Vegetation.
Nicht so bekannt, aber nicht weniger angenehm sind Wintergärten und Innenhöfe. Diese Räume werden zu Lungen des Hauses, weil sie sich im Zentrum befinden und die anderen Räume um sie herum angeordnet sind, um die Belüftung und das natürliche Licht voll zu nutzen. Genau wie im Außenbereich kann man dort einen Rasen anlegen, Blumen und sogar Bäume pflanzen, die sich den klimatischen Bedingungen und dem Boden des Innenhofes anpassen. Sie sind für Wohnungen geeignet, in denen man einen bepflanzten Raum haben möchte, obwohl er sich im Inneren befindet, und der vom Schlafzimmer, vom Bad oder von irgendeinem anderen Ort aus zugänglich ist.
Diese Art von Gestaltung schafft nicht nur eine natürliche Umgebung innerhalb des Zuhauses, sondern sorgt zusätzlich dafür, dass die Luft durch die Pflanzen gereinigt wird.

Terrassen zijn ideale plaatsen om te worden omgevormd tot kleine boomgaarden, waar niet alleen de keuze van de soorten, maar ook het ontwerp van de meubels en versieringen zorgen voor een eigen stijl. Alvorens te beginnen met planten, moet gekeken worden naar de eigenschappen van het terras, de mate waarin de planten zich aanpassen aan de omgeving en de werkelijk beschikbare ruimte. Op die manier kan een terras worden omgevormd tot een kleine, aangename en elegante tuin. Op terrassen die op het oosten liggen kunnen vrijwel alle gewassen worden verbouwd, omdat de zon die er komt zwak is en geen schade aan de plant veroorzaakt. Als het terras daarentegen op het noorden ligt, moet er worden gekozen voor planten die weinig zonlicht nodig hebben.
Patio's zijn veelal kleine ruimtes die geen direct zonlicht ontvangen en daardoor geschikt zijn voor soorten die het goed doen in de schaduw of halfschaduw. Een goede inrichting biedt intimiteit en gezelligheid.
Balkons zijn vaak onbenutte ruimtes en hebben meestal een klein oppervlak. Ze kunnen desondanks worden omgevormd tot een verlengstuk van het interieur en verbeteren op die manier niet alleen het uitzicht, maar vormen ook een gezellige etalage met overvloedige begroeiing.
Niet zo bekend maar daarom niet minder aangenaam zijn binnentuinen en binnenplaatsen. Dergelijke ruimtes zijn een groene long van de woning omdat ze in het midden liggen en de overige vertrekken en rondom zijn ingericht, zodat maximaal kan worden geprofiteerd van ventilatie en hemellicht. Als buitenvertrek kunnen ze ook gazon, bloemen en zelfs bomen hebben, die zijn aangepast aan de klimatologische omstandigheden en het terrein van de patio. Ze zijn geschikt voor woningen waar men wil genieten van een groene ruimte, ook al is dat binnen, met toegang vanuit een slaapkamer, een badkamer of vanuit een willekeurig ander vertrek.
Dit soort ruimtes valt niet alleen op door het vermogen om een natuurlijke omgeving binnenin de woning te creëren, maar ook vanwege de eigenschap van planten om de lucht te zuiveren.

I terrazzi sono spazi che si prestano facilmente ad essere trasformati in piccoli verzieri, dove, oltre ad avere una grande importanza le specie scelte, diventano determinati sia il design dei mobili che gli ornamenti che conferiscono allo spazio uno stile singolare. Prima d'iniziare la coltivazione delle piante, è importante studiare le proprietà del terrazzo e gli aspetti ambientali in modo tale da poterlo adattare all'ambiente circostante ed al suo effettivo spazio. In questo modo sarà possibile trasformare il terrazzo in un piccolo, piacevole ed elegante giardino. Nei terrazzi esposti ad est è possibile coltivare quasi tutto giacché ricevono una delicata esposizione di luce solare che non danneggia le piante. Per i terrazzi esposti a nord, invece, è consigliabile scegliere piante che necessitano di un'esposizione solare meno prolungata.

I cortili, che sono in genere spazi più ridotti dove il sole non incide in maniera così diretta, possono accogliere, invece, specie che crescono bene all'ombra o in penombra. Se ben pianificati possono diventare spazi molto intimi ed accoglienti.

I balconi, che spesso sono spazi sprecati e constano di pochi metri quadrati, possono, invece, trasformarsi in una prolungazione dello spazio interno, permettendo di godere di piacevoli vedute e di disporre di una vetrina accogliente dalla rigogliosa vegetazione.

Non così conosciuti ma non meno piacevoli sono i giardini ed i cortili interni. Questi spazi diventano dei veri e propri polmoni della casa perché sono situati al centro ed il resto delle stanze sono distribuite attorno al loro perimetro per sfruttare al massimo la ventilazione e laluce naturale. Come uno spazio esterno, il cortile può avere prato verde, fiori e addirittura alberi che si adattano alle condizioni climatiche del terreno del cortile. Sono adatti alle abitazioni in cui si desidera godere di uno spazio verde, nonostante sia interno, al quale è possibile accedere da una stanza da letto, da un bagno o da qualunque altro punto della casa.

Questo tipo d'interventi spiccano non soltanto per la loro capacità di creare un ambiente naturale all'interno dell'abitazione ma anche per la proprietà propria delle piante di purificare l'aria.

La terraza es un espacio idóneo para transformarlo en un pequeño jardín; en él no sólo son importantes las especies elegidas sino también el diseño del mobiliario y los ornamentos, que darán un estilo propio. Antes de plantar, hay que estudiar las propiedades de la terraza y los aspectos ambientales para poder adaptarla a su entorno y a su espacio real. De este modo, se conseguirá transformarla en un pequeño vergel agradable y elegante. En las terrazas orientadas hacia el este se puede cultivar una gran diversidad de especies, ya que el sol que reciben es suave y no causa daño a las plantas. Por el contrario, si la terraza está orientada hacia el norte habrá que escoger plantas que requieran menos luz.

Los patios suelen ser zonas más reducidas donde el sol no incide tan directamente y, por lo tanto, admiten especies que viven bien en sombra o semisombra. Si se planifican bien pueden resultar muy íntimos y acogedores.

Los balcones suelen ser espacios desaprovechados, en muchos casos con pocos metros cuadrados. Sin embargo, pueden transformarse en la prolongación del espacio interior y conseguir de este modo no sólo mejorar las vistas sino también disponer de un escaparate acogedor y de vegetación abundante.

No tan conocidos pero no menos agradables son los jardines y patios interiores. Este tipo de espacios se convierten en los pulmones de la casa porque se sitúan en el centro y el resto de estancias se distribuyen alrededor de su perímetro para aprovechar al máximo la ventilación y la luz natural. Igual que un espacio exterior, pueden contar con césped, flores e incluso árboles que se adaptan a las condiciones climatológicas y del terreno del patio. Son adecuados para aquellas viviendas que quieren disfrutar de un espacio vegetado aún estando situados en el interior, con acceso desde un dormitorio, desde un cuarto de baño o desde cualquier otro punto.

Este tipo de intervenciones destacan no sólo por su capacidad de crear un entorno natural dentro de la vivienda sino también por la propiedad que tienen las plantas de purificar el aire.

Arborètum
Barcelona, Spain

Canopies, pergolas and awnings mean that we can enjoy the outdoors with the shade that we require. Retractable canopies are ideal when you want total shade, and they can be removed when you want to enjoy the sun.

Met zonweringen, pergola's en zonneschermen kan men buiten genieten van de nodige schaduw. Oprolbare zonneschermen zijn ideaal als om een schaduwzone te creëren. Ze kunnen later worden opgerold om van de zon te genieten.

Mit Hilfe von Markisen, Pergolas und Schutzdächern, die den notwendigen Schatten spenden, können wir den Aufenthalt im Freien genießen. Aufrollbare Marquisen sind ideal, wenn ein Bereich vollständig im Schatten liegen soll. Wenn man die Sonne genießen will, kann man sie einfach aufrollen.

Le tende per esterno, le pergole e le tettoie permetteranno di sfruttare lo spazio esterno fornendoci l'ombreggiatura necessaria. Le tende avvolgibili da esterno sono l'ideale quando ciò che si cerca è una zona completamente in ombra; inoltre, si possono ritirare quando vogliamo godere del sole.

Les stores, les pergolas et les marquises permettront de profiter de l'extérieur en fournissant l'ombre nécessaire. Les stores bannes enroulables sont idéals lorsque l'on souhaite créer une zone complètement ombragée. Très pratiques, il suffit de les replier pour profiter du soleil.

Los toldos, las pérgolas y las marquesinas permitirán disfrutar del exterior aportándonos la sombra necesaria. Los toldos enrollables son ideales cuando lo que se busca es una zona de sombra total, y se pueden retirar cuando queremos disfrutar del sol.

If the terrace is big enough, separate it into two spaces: a lounge/dining room to spend many hours with friends, and a sun terrace to enjoy the sun in summer. A striking swimming pool is the best accessory to survive high temperatures.

Wenn die Terrasse groß genug ist, können wir sie in zwei Bereiche unterteilen: Einen Wohn- und Essbereich für lange Abende mit Gästen und einen Bereich zum Sonnenbaden. Ein großartiger Swimmingpool ist ideal, um hohe Temperaturen auszuhalten.

Si les dimensions de la terrasse le permettent, il est possible de découper l'espace en deux ambiances : une zone de salon-salle à manger destinée à la convivialité et une zone solarium pour profiter du soleil en été. Une superbe piscine sera le complément parfait pour supporter les hautes températures.

Als de afmetingen van het terras het toelaten kunnen we twee verschillende entourages van elkaar scheiden: een gedeelte voor een eet- en zithoek om gezellig samen te zijn en een solarium om van de zomerzon te genieten. Een fantastisch zwembad is de beste aanvulling hierop, voor verkoeling op warme dagen.

Se le dimensioni della terrazza lo permettono, possiamo dividere i due ambienti: una zona soggiorno-pranzo dove passare ore conversando e una zona solarium, per godere del sole d'estate. Una magnifica piscina sarà il miglior completamento per far fronte alle alte temperature.

Si las dimensiones de la terraza lo permiten, podemos separar dos ambientes: una zona de estar-comedor donde pasar largas horas de tertulia, y una zona de solárium, para disfrutar del sol en verano. Una magnífica piscina será el mejor complemento para soportar las altas temperaturas.

Arborètum
Barcelona, Spain

Latticeworks are used mainly in urban terraces, as from the roof of other buildings the inside of the terrace can be seen. Windbreaks can be used with latticework to close areas heavily exposed to air, such as pergolas, gazebos or outdoor dining areas.

Zonneschermen worden met name op terrassen in stadswoningen gebruikt, aangezien men vanaf het dakterras van andere gebouwen naar binnen kan kijken. Windschermen kunnen worden afgewisseld met jaloezieën die ook beschutting bieden tegen de wind, zoals bijvoorbeeld pergola's, prieeltjes of eethoeken in de open lucht.

Jalousien werden vor allem auf Terrassen in der Stadt benutzt, da man von den Dachterrassen der anderen Gebäude hinein sehen kann. Man kann Windschutzzäune oder Jalousien anbringen, um Bereiche, die dem Wind zu sehr ausgesetzt sind, wie z.B. Pergolas, Pavillons oder Essplätze im Freien, abzuschließen.

La griglia per rampicanti è un elemento che si utilizza soprattutto sulle terrazze urbane, dal momento che dal tetto degli altri edifici si può altrimenti vedere all'interno. Si possono alternare barriere antivento con le griglie per chiudere zone che non devono essere troppo esposte all'aria, come ad esempio pergole, gazebo o tavoli da pranzo all'aria aperta.

Les treillages sont principalement utilisés sur les terrasses urbaines pour éviter les regards indiscrets depuis les toitures-terrasses des bâtiments annexes. Les paravents peuvent être installés en alternance avec des treillages pour clôturer les zones excessivement exposées à l'air comme les pergolas, les tonnelles ou les zones de repas extérieures, par exemple.

Las celosías se utilizan sobre todo en las terrazas urbanas, ya que evitan que desde la azotea de otros edificios se pueda ver el interior. Los cortavientos pueden alternarse con celosías para cerrar zonas demasiado expuestas al aire, como por ejemplo pérgolas, gacebos o comedores al aire libre

Arborètum
Barcelona, Spain

Arborètum
Barcelona, Spain

Arborètum
Barcelona, Spain

Once you know what areas receive the most pleasant shade, you can strategically locate the areas destined for relaxation, whether under the shade of a tree or in a shady corner at dusk.

Als eenmaal duidelijk is wat de beste schaduwzones zijn, kunnen we bepalen wat de strategische plekken zijn voor ontspanning, hetzij in de schaduw van een boom of aan het einde van de middag in een schaduwrijk hoekje.

Wenn wir herausgefunden haben, welche Schattenzonen am angenehmsten sind, können wir die strategischen Punkte für die Erholung festlegen, entweder im Schatten eines Baumes oder in einer schattigen Ecke in der Abenddämmerung.

Una volta che siano state individuate le migliori zone d'ombra, si possono posizionare i punti strategici destinati al riposo, sotto un albero o in angolo in ombra il pomeriggio.

Après avoir étudié les zones d'ombre les plus agréables, il est possible de définir les points stratégiques destinés à la relaxation, en les plaçants à l'ombre d'un arbre ou dans un coin ombragé en fin de journée.

Una vez hayamos estudiado cuáles son las zonas de sombra más agradables, podremos situar los puntos estratégicos destinados al descanso, ya sea bajo la sombra de un árbol o en un rincón umbrío al atardecer.

Arborètum
Barcelona, Spain

There are a wide variety of floors for terraces. Choosing a floor which is easy to clean, maintain and which is resistant, is one of the most important decisions. If you choose wood for flooring, specify that it is for outdoor use because it varies in size depending on the humidity.

Er bestaat een grote verscheidenheid aan terrasvloeren. Kies voor een vloer die eenvoudig kan worden schoongemaakt, onderhoudsvriendelijk en resistent is. Als de keuze valt op een houten vloer, dan moet het hout speciaal voor buiten zijn, anders kan het door de warmte krimpen en uitzetten.

Es gibt viele verschiedene Terrassenböden. Eine der wichtigsten Entscheidungen ist es, einen widerstandsfähigen Boden zu wählen, der leicht zu reinigen und zu pflegen ist. Wenn wir Holz als Bodenbelag wählen, muss es für draußen geeignet sein, weil es sich sonst auf Grund der Feuchtigkeit verziehen kann.

Esiste una grande varietà di pavimentazioni da terrazza. Sceglierne una facile da pulire, da mantenere e che sia resistente sarà una delle mosse più importanti. Se scegliamo legno per il parquet, dovrà essere specifico per esterni perché altrimenti subirà dilatazioni in funzione dell'umidità.

Il existe une grande variété de sols pour terrasses. Il est indispensable de choisir un sol résistant, facile à nettoyer et à entretenir. Si l'on opte pour un parquet en bois, celui-ci doit être spécialement conçu pour les espaces extérieurs. Dans le cas contraire, il risque de rétrécir ou de prendre de l'extension sous l'effet de l'humidité.

Existe una gran variedad de suelos para terrazas. Elegir un suelo fácil de limpiar, de mantener y que sea resistente supondrá una de las decisiones más importantes. Si escogemos madera para el entarimado, deberá ser específica para exteriores porque sino puede encogerse y dilatarse a causa de la humedad.

Arborètum
Barcelona, Spain

237

Arborètum
Barcelona, Spain

Courtyards are typically enclosed spaces between common walls, they can be as customized as you wish as they are independent and have little connection with neighboring gardens.

Patio's kunnen, omdat ze afgesloten zijn en normaal gesproken tussen gemeenschappelijke muren liggen, zo gepersonaliseerd worden als we willen, omdat ze onafhankelijk zijn en niet in verbinding staan met de aanliggende tuinen.

Da Innenhöfe geschlossene Räume sind, die sich normalerweise zwischen Scheidemauern befinden, kann man sie so persönlich gestalten, wie man will. Sie sind unabhängig und haben wenig mit den benachbarten Gärten zu tun.

Il cortile, essendo di solito uno spazio chiuso e delimitato da elementi divisori, può essere progettato in assoluta libertà visto che acquista un'identità indipendente e non è in relazione con i giardini vicini.

Les cours, espaces fermés et normalement situés entre des murs mitoyens, peuvent être aménagées à notre guise car elles se développent de façon indépendante sans besoin d'homogénéité avec les jardins voisins.

Los patios, al ser espacios cerrados y normalmente entre medianeras, se pueden diseñar todo lo personalizados que queramos, ya que actúan de forma independiente y guardan poca relación con los jardines vecinos.

Arborètum
Barcelona, Spain
(left)

This back courtyard of a ground floor was turned into a space with three distinct areas: a dining room, garden and a covered study. Due to topographical conditions, the different spaces were constructed in a terraced manner, as originally it was a sunken courtyard, with a profound slope from the house.

Deze achterpatio van een woning op de begane grond is omgevormd tot een ruimte met drie verschillende zones: een eethoek, een tuin en een overdekte werkkamer. Vanwege de topografische omstandigheden is gekozen voor verschillende entourages, omdat de patio een beetje verzonken lag ten opzichte van de woning.

Dieser Hinterhof eines Erdgeschosses wurde in einen Raum mit drei verschiedenen Bereichen aufgeteilt: Essbereich, Garten und überdachtes Studio. Aufgrund der topografischen Bedingungen wurden die verschiedenen Zonen stufenförmig gestaltet, da es sich um einen vertieften Innenhof mit einem großen Höhenunterschied zur Wohnung handelt.

Questo cortile sul retro al piano terra è stato trasformato in uno spazio con tre diverse zone: un tavolo da pranzo, un giardino e uno studio con copertura. A causa della topografia del terreno, con il cortile posto molto più basso dell'abitazione, i diversi ambienti sono stati ubicati su gradoni ad altezza diversa.

Cette arrière-cour d'un rez-de-chaussée a été convertie en un espace découpé en trois zones distinctes : une zone repas, un jardin et un studio couvert. Pour des raisons topographiques – une cour enfoncée sur un terrain dénivelé – on a aménagé ces espaces en terrasses échelonnées.

Este patio trasero de una planta baja se convirtió en un espacio con tres zonas diferenciadas: un comedor, un jardín y un estudio cubierto. Por las condiciones topográficas, los distintos ambientes se colocaron de forma escalonada, ya que se trataba de un patio hundido, con un profundo desnivel desde la vivienda.

Arborètum
Barcelona, Spain

Ipe decking can help you to enhance different areas in the courtyard. For example, a relaxation area with a bench or an area with a table and chairs to have a coffee. If the platform consists of two platforms superimposed on each other, a change of direction of the decking will create two different levels.

Met een ipé-houten vloer kunnen er verschillende zones in de patio worden geaccentueerd: bijvoorbeeld een relaxzone met een bank of een zitje met een tafel en stoelen om koffie te drinken. Als de houten vloer op een onderlaag steunt, dan kunnen er met een wijziging in de oriëntatie van de latten twee verschillende niveaus worden gecreëerd.

Mit Hilfe eines Podests aus Ipe-Holz kann man verschiedene Bereiche des Innenhofes hervorheben, zum Beispiel eine Ruhezone mit einer Bank oder einen Bereich mit einem Tisch und Stühlen zum Kaffeetrinken. Wenn das Podest auf einem anderen aufliegt und die Leisten in eine andere Richtung zeigen, erhält man zwei verschiedene Ebenen.

Con la collocazione di un calpestabile in assi legno di ipè potrete rialzare alcune zone del giardino. Per esempio una zona relax con una panchina o un tavolo con sedie per prendere il caffè. Se questa pedana è appoggiata su un'altra, con un diverso orientamento delle assi si creeranno due differenti livelli.

L'installation de caillebotis en ipé permet de mettre en valeur différentes zones de la cour. Un espace de détente avec un banc ou un autre équipé d'une table et de chaises pour prendre un café, par exemple. En superposant les caillebotis, et en changeant d'orientation les planches, on parvient à créer deux niveaux distincts.

Con la disposición de una tarima de ipé podrás realzar diferentes zonas en el patio. Por ejemplo, una zona de relax con un banco o una zona con una mesa y sillas para tomar café. Si la tarima se apoya en otra superpuesta a la anterior, con un cambio de orientación en los listones conseguirás crear dos niveles diferenciados.

Arborètum
Barcelona, Spain

Arborètum
Barcelona, Spain

Arborètum
Barcelona, Spain

Balcony plants should be watered almost daily because warm air and sunshine quickly dry the soil.

Planten op het balkon moeten praktisch iedere dag water krijgen, omdat de grond snel uitdroogt door de warme lucht en de zon.

Balkonpflanzen muss man praktisch täglich gießen, weil warme Luft und lange Sonnenstunden die Erde schnell austrocknen.

Le piante del balcone devono essere innaffiate quotidianamente perché l'aria calda e le ore di solleone seccano rapidamente il terreno.

Les plantes du balcon doivent être arrosées pratiquement tous les jours car l'air chaud et les heures de soleil assèchent rapidement la terre.

Las plantas del balcón deben regarse prácticamente a diario porque el aire caliente y las horas de sol secan rápidamente la tierra.

Arborètum
Barcelona, Spain

Arborètum
Barcelona, Spain

If you have enough space, convert the balcony into a meeting space by moving the living area outdoors. To create an intimate and personal space and enjoy tranquil moments, the best option is to place a table and chairs or just an armchair to rest.

Als de ruimte het toelaat kunt u het balkon omtoveren tot een gezellig hoekje door de zitkamer naar buiten te verplaatsen. Voor een intieme en persoonlijke ruimte en om te genieten van rustige momenten kunt u het beste een tafel en stoelen neerzetten, of gewoon een luie stoel om in uit te rusten.

Wenn der Balkon groß genug ist, können wir ihn zu einem Treffpunkt machen und das Wohnzimmer nach draußen verlegen. Um einen intimen und persönlichen Ort zu gestalten und Augenblicke der Ruhe zu genießen, ist es am besten, einen Tisch und ein paar Stühle oder einfach einen Sessel zum Ausruhen aufzustellen.

Se lo spazio lo permette, possiamo trasformare il balcone in un luogo di ritrovo trasferendo la zona giorno all'esterno. Per creare uno spazio intimo e tranquillo e godersi momenti di relax, la migliore opzione è collocare sul balcone un tavolo e alcune sedie, o semplicemente una poltrona in cui poter riposare.

Si l'espace le permet, il est possible de convertir le balcon en un lieu de réunion en déplaçant la zone de vie à l'extérieur. Pour créer un espace intime et personnel, ainsi que pour profiter de moments de tranquillité, le meilleur moyen consiste à installer une table et des chaises, ou tout simplement un fauteuil pour se reposer.

Si el espacio lo permite, podemos convertir el balcón en un espacio de reunión trasladando la zona de estar al exterior. Para crear un espacio íntimo y personal y disfrutar de momentos de tranquilidad, la mejor opción es colocar una mesa y unas sillas o simplemente una butaca donde poder descansar.

Arborètum
Barcelona, Spain

For extremely sunny days, you need a little shade. A parasol will give the necessary shade for cookouts.

Op zonnige dagen is schaduw nodig. Een parasol helpt om een beschermde ruimte te creëren om buiten te kunnen eten.

Für Tage mit zu viel Sonne braucht man ein bisschen Schatten. Ein Sonnenschirm bietet einen geschützten Ort für das Essen im Freien.

Nei giorni di sole eccessivo, c'è bisogno di un po' d'ombra. Un ombrellone servirà a creare uno spazio protetto per poter mangiare all'aperto.

Un peu d'ombre s'avère nécessaire lors des journées trop ensoleillées. Un parasol permettra de créer un espace protégé pour manger en plein air.

Para los días con demasiado sol, se necesita un poco de sombra. Una sombrilla ayudará a crear un espacio protegido para poder comer al aire libre.

Arborètum
Barcelona, Spain

One of the most important aspects in balconies is the total weight. Choose lighter containers made from material such as wicker. It can be a lot more peaceful and pretty to choose a small number of large pots than dozens of small pots.

Een van de belangrijkste aspecten van balkons is het totale gewicht. Het beste zijn lichtgewicht of rieten bakken of potten. Een beperkt aantal grote potten kan rustiger en mooier zijn dan tientallen kleine bloempotten.

Ein wichtiger Aspekt, der bei Balkonen zu beachten ist, ist das Gesamtgewicht. Am besten wählt man Gefäße oder Blumentöpfe aus leichtem Material oder Korb. Wenige große Blumenkästen können viel beruhigender und hübscher wirken als Dutzende kleiner Blumentöpfe.

Uno degli aspetti più importanti del balcone è il suo peso complessivo. È preferibile scegliere contenitori e vasi di vimini o di materiale leggero. Può risultare molto più ordinato e gradevole usare pochi vasi grandi piuttosto che decine di piccoli contenitori.

Il est très important de respecter le poids maximal pour un balcon. Mieux vaut choisir des récipients ou des pots fabriqués dans des matériaux légers ou dans de l'osier. Le choix d'un nombre réduit de grands pots peut s'avérer plus apaisant et joli que des dizaines de petits pots.

Uno de los aspectos importantes en los balcones es el peso total. Lo mejor es elegir contenedores o macetas de materiales poco pesados como el mimbre. Un reducido número de macetas grandes en lugar de decenas de tiestos pequeños pueden dar un aspecto más relajado y bonito al balcón.

Arborètum
Barcelona, Spain

Arborètum
Barcelona, Spain

This outdoors living area is an example of minimalist exterior design in a balcony without any major fuss. Only a few plants were planted in strategic locations so as not to compete with the true protagonist: the landscape.

Für dieses Wohnzimmer im Freien auf einem Balkon wurde ein minimalistisches, zurückhaltendes Design gewählt. Man hat sich für wenige Pflanzen entschieden, die an strategischen Stellen aufgestellt wurden, um nicht mit dem wahren Hauptdarsteller zu konkurrieren: der Landschaft.

Cette salle de séjour de plein air est un exemple de décoration d'extérieur sur un balcon laissant place au minimalisme sans excentricité. Les quelques incursions végétales placées dans des endroits stratégiques ne cherchent pas à rivaliser avec l'acteur principal des lieux : le paysage.

In deze salon op een balkon in de open lucht is gekozen voor een minimalistisch ontwerp, waarbij felle kleuren zijn gemeden. Er is gekozen voor enkele plantaardige elementen op strategische plekken, die niet concurreren met de werkelijke hoofdrolspeler: het landschap.

Questo soggiorno all'aria aperta è un esempio di exterior design riuscito in uno spazio caratterizzato da un minimalismo discreto. Si è optato per pochi tocchi di verde posizionati nei punti strategici per non mettere in ombra il vero protagonista: il paesaggio.

En esta sala de estar en un balcón al aire libre se ha apostado por un diseño minimalista y sin estridencias. Se ha optado por unos pocos elementos vegetales situados en lugares estratégicos para no competir con el verdadero protagonista: el paisaje.

Arborètum
Barcelona, Spain

Arborètum
Barcelona, Spain

Arborètum
Barcelona, Spain

Miró Rivera Architects
Austin, TX, USA
(this page)

Arborètum
Barcelona, Spain
(this page)

Hanging gardens and several types of plants, including vines, can be placed on platforms at various levels.

Hangende tuinen en verschillende soorten planten, zoals klimplanten, kunnen op platforms op verschillende niveaus worden geplaatst.

Auf Podesten in verschiedenen Höhen kann man hängende Gärten und verschiedene Pflanzenarten, wie Kletterpflanzen, anbringen.

I giardini pensili e molti tipi di piante, come i rampicanti, si possono posizionare su piattaforme a diversi livelli.

Jardins suspendus et plusieurs types de plantes, comme les espèces grimpantes, peuvent être placés sur des plates-formes distribuées sur plusieurs niveaux.

En plataformas a distintos niveles se pueden colocar jardines colgantes y varios tipos de plantas, como trepadoras.

John Henry Architects
Melbourne, Australia

276

On the ground floor where the living room and dining room are located, there is a large glass expanse that extends to both sides of the house. Through the windows you can observe nature and feel its presence inside.

Im Erdgeschoss, wo sich das Wohn- und Esszimmer befinden, wurde ein großes Fenster eingebaut, das sich über zwei Seiten des Hauses erstreckt. Durch die Fenster kann man die Natur draußen betrachten und ihre Anwesenheit drinnen spüren.

Au rez-de-chaussée, où sont situés salon et salle à manger, une grande baie vitrée qui s'étend de part et d'autre de la maison est installée. À travers elle, il est possible de contempler la nature extérieure et de sentir sa présence à l'intérieur de la demeure.

Op de begane grond, waar zich de salon en de eetkamer bevinden, is een groot raam geïnstalleerd, dat aan weerszijden van het huis uitzicht biedt. Door de ramen kan men de natuur buiten aanschouwen en zijn aanwezigheid tot binnen voelen.

Al pianterreno, dove sono collocate la sala da pranzo e il soggiorno, è stato posizionato un grande finestrone che si estende su entrambi i lati dell'abitazione. Dalle finestre è possibile osservare la natura all'esterno e sentire la sua presenza all'interno della casa.

En la planta baja, donde están situados el salón y el comedor, hay instalado un gran ventanal que se extiende a ambos lados de la casa. Por las ventanas se puede observar la naturaleza en el exterior y sentir su presencia en el interior.

Bernardes & Jacobsen Arquitectura
São Paulo, Brasil

The skylight does not only visually link the interior and exterior, it also lights up the lower garden level and prevents a claustrophobic feeling. The staircase with metal railings and bleached pine steps, leads to this interior space, which was created when the house was restructured.

Een dakraam is niet alleen een visuele verbinding tussen buiten en binnen, maar verlicht ook de lager gelegen tuin en vermindert het gevoel opgesloten te zitten. De trap met metalen leuning en gewitte grenenhouten treden, leidt naar deze binnenruimte die dankzij de renovatie van het huis is ontstaan.

Roberto Lanaro
Bassano del Grappa, Vicenza, Italy
(this page)

Das Oberlicht verbindet nicht nur den Innen- mit dem Außenbereich, sondern erhellt auch den tiefer liegenden Garten und verhindert so das Gefühl, eingeschlossen zu sein. Die Treppe mit Metallgeländer und Stufen aus gebleichtem Pinienholz führt in diesen Innenraum, der beim Umbau des Hauses geschaffen wurde.

Il lucernario non solo unisce visivamente interno ed esterno, ma illumina il giardino al livello inferiore evitando la sensazione di trovarsi in uno spazio chiuso. La scala, con passamano di metallo e scalini di legno di pino sbiancato, conduce a questo spazio interno che è stato creato in seguito alla ristrutturazione della casa.

Le puits de lumière unit non seulement l'intérieur et l'extérieur, mais il illumine également le jardin de l'étage inférieur en évitant la sensation de confinement. L'escalier, à main courante en métal et à marches en bois de pin blanchies, mène à cet espace intérieur qui fut créé lors de la restructuration de la maison.

El lucernario no solo une visualmente el interior y el exterior, sino que también ilumina el jardín del nivel inferior y evita la sensación de estar encerrado. La escalera, con pasamanos de metal y peldaños de madera de pino blanqueados, conduce a este espacio interior que se creó con la reestructuración de la casa.

Bercy Chen Studio
Austin, TX, USA
(opposite, top left)

Roberto Lanaro
Bassano del Grappa, Vicenza, Italy
(opposite, top right)

Arborètum
Barcelona, Spain
(opposite, bottom left)

Arborètum
Barcelona, Spain
(opposite, bottom right)

Courtyards can be separated from the rest of the house through sliding glass doors, which can also be fully opened and remain closed on one side.

De patio's kunnen van de rest van de woning worden afgescheiden door middel van glazen schuifpuien, die ook helemaal open kunnen en aan een van de zijkanten gesloten blijven.

Die Innenhöfe können durch Glas-Schiebetüren von der Wohnung ab getrennt werden. Diese Türen kann man vollständig öffnen oder eine der Seiten kann geschlossen bleiben.

Il cortile può essere separato dal resto della casa attraverso porte di vetro scorrevoli, che si possano aprire completamente e rimanere chiuse in una delle corsie guida.

Les cours peuvent être séparées du reste du logement au moyen de portes coulissantes en verre qui pourront ainsi être entièrement ouvertes et fermées sur l'un des côtés.

Es posible separar los patios del resto de la vivienda por medio de puertas de cristal correderas; estas también se pueden abrir completamente y permanecer cerradas en uno de los laterales.

Kenji Tagashira
Sakai, Japan

Edward Suzuki Associates
Kyoto, Japan
(opposite page)

Edward Suzuki Associates
Kyoto, Japan

Thanks to the high ceilings a few trees could be planted next to the sofas. The trunks protrude from the holes in the parquet, while the top almost reaches the ceiling.

Dank der Höhe der Decken kann man neben dem Sofa Bäume pflanzen. Die Stämme wachsen aus Aussparungen im Parkett heraus und die Kronen reichen fast bis zur Decke.

La hauteur conséquente des pièces a permis la plantation d'arbres à côté des canapés. Les troncs ressortent des trous réalisés dans le parquet, tandis que la cime des arbres atteint presque le plafond.

Ter hoogte van de plafonds konden een aantal bomen naast de sofa's worden geplant. De stammen komen uit de gaten in het parket, terwijl de kruin van de bomen bijna het plafond bereiken.

Grazie all'altezza del tetto è stato possibile piantare alberi vicino ai divani. I tronchi fuoriescono dai fori praticati nel parquet, mentre la chioma degli alberi quasi raggiunge il tetto.

Gracias a la altura de los techos se pudieron plantar unos árboles junto a los sofás. Los troncos sobresalen de los agujeros hechos en el parqué, mientras que la copa de los árboles casi alcanza el techo.

Bernardes & Jacobsen Arquitectura
São Paulo, Brasil

Skylights and courtyards have a similar function: the light comes in through the windows, lights up the interior and distributes energy.

Dakramen en patio's hebben een soortgelijke functie: het licht komt binnen door de ramen, verlicht het interieur en verdeelt de energie.

Oberlichter und Patios haben eine ähnliche Funktion: Das Licht kommt durch die Fenster herein, erhellt das Innere und liefert Energie.

I lucernari e i cortili interni hanno funzioni simili: la luce entra dalla finestra, illumina l'interno e lascia fluire la sua energia.

Les puits de lumière et les cours remplissent une fonction similaire : faire pénétrer la lumière à travers les fenêtres, illuminer l'intérieur et propager l'énergie.

Los lucernarios y patios poseen una función similar: la luz entra por las ventanas, ilumina el interior y distribuye su energía.

Some courtyards, whether for their neutral colors, the use of sand or the simplicity of their appearance, become an oasis of calm.

Sommige patio's veranderen, hetzij door de neutrale kleuren, het gebruik van zand of de eenvoud van het ontwerp, in een oase van rust.

Manche Innenhöfe verwandeln sich aufgrund ihrer neutralen Farben, durch den Gebrauch von Sand oder durch ihr schlichtes Aussehen in Oasen der Ruhe.

Alcuni cortili, per i colori neutri o per la semplicità del loro aspetto, si sanno trasformare in oasi di tranquillità.

Certaines cours, par leurs couleurs neutres, par l'utilisation de sable ou encore par la simplicité de leur apparence, deviennent de véritables havres de paix.

Algunos patios, ya sea por sus colores neutros, por el uso de arena o por la simplicidad de su apariencia, se convierten en un oasis de calma.

Arborètum
Barcelona, Spain
(left)

Outdoor furniture, lighting and accessories

Gartenmöbel, Beleuchtung und Zubehör

Mobilier de jardin, éclairage et accessoires

Tuinmeubels, verlichting en accessoires

Mobili da esterni, illuminazione ed accessori

Mobiliario exterior, iluminación y accesorios

Furniture suffers a lot outside, even furniture suitable for outdoor use. Currently the trend is the use of low maintenance materials and furniture for relaxation. Natural materials such as teak, wicker and stone can be a good option.

The ideal location for the furniture in the garden is in a sunny location, provided that they resist high temperatures and foundations for the furniture is a good idea so that it does not sink into the lawn. Moisture is one of the main causes of the deterioration of furniture. However, even if we opt for excellent quality, sturdy furniture, we should care for it on a daily basis or at least regularly. The garden lighting should be planned taking into account the layout of the space and, above all, with respect for nature. The latest features are low lights and solar lights with LED. When distributing the points of light, decide what use each zone will have. To achieve adequate light in porches or summerhouses opt for ceiling lights, lampposts or high lighting fixtures.

To finish off the garden ambience, incorporate small decorative details that add charm and help personalize the space. The type of accessories depends on the style you want to achieve and the composition after choosing plants and having designed the form of the paths and stone areas. Opt for decorative pots, fixed stone globes, statues, fountains, among many other options. If you are looking for a more rural space, install birdbaths and birdhouses. To attract butterflies and hummingbirds place allusive motifs on stones to attract their attention, as decorative features. All accessories will turn the garden into a space adapted to personal taste and will provide the final touch to this wild corner of the house.

Möbel leiden im Freien sehr, selbst wenn sie speziell dafür hergestellt wurden. Zurzeit geht der Trend hin zu Materialen, die wenig Pflege erfordern, und zu Möbeln, die der Entspannung dienen. Natürliche Materialien wie Teak, Rattan und Stein sind eine gute Wahl.

Der ideale Standort für Gartenmöbel ist ein sonniger Platz, vorausgesetzt, dass sie hohe Temperaturen vertragen. Wenn möglich sollte der Bereich zementiert sein, um zu vermeiden, dass die Tisch- und Stuhlbeine in den Rasen einsinken. Feuchtigkeit ist eine der Hauptursachen für die Abnutzung der Möbel. Deshalb müssen wir sie, auch wenn wir uns für widerstandsfähige Möbel von ausgezeichneter Qualität entscheiden, täglich oder zumindest regelmäßig pflegen.

Bei der Planung der Gartenbeleuchtung muss man die Aufteilung des Bereichs beachten und vor allem Rücksicht auf die Natur nehmen. Zu den neuesten Einsatzmöglichkeiten zählen gedämpfte Lichtquellen und LED-Solarlampen. Bei der Verteilung der Lichtquellen muss man entscheiden, welchem Zweck jeder Bereich dienen soll. Für ein angemessenes zentrales Licht auf Veranden und in Lauben kann man Deckenlampen oder Hängeleuchten in Form von Laternen oder hoch angebrachten Wandlampen wählen.

Um das Ambiente im Garten zu vervollständigen, kann man kleine dekorative Elemente anbringen, die fröhlich wirken und zur persönlichen Gestaltung des Außenbereichs beitragen. Die Art der Accessoires hängt vom gewünschten Stil sowie von der Komposition der Pflanzen und der Gestaltung der Wege und der gepflasterten Bereiche ab.

Man kann aus dekorativen Blumentöpfen, Steinkugeln, Statuen, Brunnen und vielen weiteren Möglichkeiten wählen. Wenn man eine ländlichere Umgebung schaffen möchte, kann man Vogelbäder oder Vogelhäuschen aufstellen. Um Schmetterlinge und Kolibris anzulocken, kann man beziehungsreiche Motive wie dekorative Figuren auf Steinen anbringen. Accessoires verleihen dem Garten einen persönlichen Stil und vervollständigen diese wilde Ecke des Hauses.

Les meubles subissent beaucoup de dommages à l'extérieur, y compris ceux destinés à cet usage. La tendance actuelle est la prédominance de matériaux requérant peu d'entretien et de mobiliers de détente. Le teck, l'osier et la pierre peuvent être une bonne option.

L'emplacement idéal pour le mobilier de jardin est un lieu ensoleillé, du moment qu'il résiste aux températures élevées, et si possible cimenté, afin d'éviter que les pieds ne s'enfoncent dans la pelouse. L'humidité est l'une des causes principales de détérioration des meubles. Toutefois, même si vous optez pour des meubles résistants et d'excellente qualité, il vous faudra leur prodiguer des soins quotidiens ou au moins réguliers.

L'éclairage du jardin doit être prévu en fonction de l'agencement de l'espace et, surtout, en mettant l'accent sur le respect de la nature. Parmi les dernières tendances les lumières ténues et les lampions solaires ou à LED. Avant de répartir les points d'éclairage, il faut déterminer l'usage qui sera attribué à chaque zone. Afin d'obtenir une lumière zénithale sous les porches ou tonnelles, il est possible d'opter pour des plafonniers ou des éclairages descendants, au moyen de réverbères ou d'appliques hautes.

Pour compléter l'atmosphère du jardin, il est possible d'y incorporer de petits détails décoratifs qui lui apporteront du charme et aideront à personnaliser l'espace extérieur. Le type d'accessoires dépendra du style souhaité et de la composition obtenue après avoir choisi les plantes et planifié la forme des sentiers et des zones en pierre.

Il est possible d'opter pour des petits pots décoratifs, des globes en pierre, des statues, des fontaines, entre autres options. Si l'on recherche un espace plus champêtre, il est également possible d'y intégrer un point d'eau pour les oiseaux ou une volière. Afin d'attirer les papillons ou les oiseaux, des motifs allusifs placés sur les pierres sont une bonne solution pour attirer leur attention, comme avec des figurines décoratives par exemple. Tous les accessoires feront du jardin un espace adapté aux goûts de chacun et apporteront une touche finale à ce petit coin sauvage de la maison.

Meubels die buiten staan hebben veel te lijden, zelfs als ze voor exterieur bedoeld zijn. Binnen de huidige trend overheersen onderhoudsvriendelijke materialen en relaxmeubelen. Natuurlijke materialen zoals teakhout, riet en steen kunnen een goede optie zijn.

De ideale plaats voor tuinmeubilair is een zonnige plek, mits de meubels bestand zijn tegen hoge temperaturen en, zo mogelijk en harde ondergrond staan, om te voorkomen dat de poten wegzakken in het gazon. Vocht is een van de belangrijkste oorzaken waardoor de meubels worden aangetast. Ook als we kiezen voor resistente meubels van eersteklas kwaliteit moeten ze dagelijks of tenminste regelmatig worden onderhouden.

Bij de keuze voor tuinverlichting moet rekening worden gehouden met de ruimte en vooral met het milieu. De laatste trends zijn zwakke verlichting, zonnelampen en LED-lampen. Bij de verdeling van de lichtpunten moet duidelijk zijn welk gebruik e aan iedere zone wordt gegeven. Voor een geschikte lichtinval op veranda's of in prieeltjes kan worden gekozen voor plafondlampen of voor naar beneden gerichte verlichting door lantaarns of hoge wandlampen.

Om de sfeer in de tuin compleet te maken is er nog de mogelijkheid om kleine decoratieve details toe te voegen, die zorgen voor charme en helpen om de buitenruimte te personaliseren. Het soort accessoires hangt af van de gewenste stijl en van de compositie die ontstaan is na het kiezen van de planten en de inrichting van paden en stenenzones.

Er zijn legio mogelijkheden, zoals decoratieve bloempotten, vaste stenen potten, beelden of fonteinen. Voor een landelijkere sfeer zijn vogelbadjes of volières een mogelijkheid. Om vlinders en kolibries te trekken, kunnen er bepaalde motieven op stenen worden aangebracht waarmee hun aandacht wordt getrokken, Dankzij deze accessoires verandert de tuin in een ruimte die aan de persoonlijke smaak is aangepast: ze zijn de finishing touch van dit wilde hoekje van het huis.

I mobili da esterni soffrono per le inclemenze del tempo anche se appositamente trattati. La tendenza attuale predominante è quella di ricorrere a materiali che richiedano una manutenzione minima e mobili da relax. Materiali naturali quali il tek, il vimine e la pietra costituiscono di solito una buona soluzione.

L'ubicazione ideale per i mobili da giardino, sempre che resistano alle alte temperature, è un luogo soleggiato che, nei limiti del possibile, dovrebbe essere cementato per evitare che le gambe sprofondino nel prato verde. L'umidità è una delle principali cause del deterioramento dei mobili da esterni, quindi, sebbene si opti per mobili resistenti e di eccellente qualità, sono necessari interventi di manutenzione giornaliera o, quanto meno, costanti.

L'illuminazione del giardino deve essere pianificata tenendo conto della distribuzione dello spazio ma, soprattutto, dando priorità al rispetto verso la natura. Tra le ultime tendenze in questo campo troviamo le luci tenui, le lampade solari e quelle a LED. Nel distribuire i punti luce, è necessario decidere quale uso assegnare ad ogni zona. Per ottenere una luce zenitale adeguata nei portici o nei chioschi si possono scegliere lampade da soffitto o optare per l'illuminazione discendente con fanali o applique alti.

Per completare l'ambiente, nel giardino è possibile inserire piccoli particolari decorativi che abbelliscono ed aiutano a personalizzare lo spazio esterno. La scelta degli accessori dipenderà dallo stile che s'intende creare e dall'ambiente ottenuto dopo aver scelto le piante ed aver pianificato la forma dei sentieri e le zone in pietra.

Tra le tante possibilità che offre il mercato si può optare per vasi decorativi, sfere di pietra, statue e fontanelle. Se s'intende creare uno spazio dall'aria più campestre, è possibile sistemare vasche per uccelli o uccelliere. Per attirare farfalle e colibrì, invece, è possibile collocare dei motivi simbolico-allusivi come figure decorative su alcune pietre. L'insieme degli accessori farà del giardino uno spazio in accordo al gusto personale, dando all'angolo silvestre della casa il tocco finale.

Los muebles sufren mucho en el exterior, incluso los que están preparados para ello. Actualmente la tendencia son los materiales que requieren poco mantenimiento y el mobiliario de relax. Materiales naturales como la teca, el mimbre y la piedra pueden ser una buena opción.

La ubicación ideal para los muebles de jardín es un lugar soleado, siempre que resistan altas temperaturas, y a ser posible que esté cimentado para evitar que las patas se hundan en el césped. La humedad es una de las principales causas del deterioro de los muebles. Sin embargo, aunque optemos por muebles resistentes y de excelente calidad, debemos brindarles un cuidado diario o, al menos, regular.

La iluminación del jardín debe planificarse teniendo en cuenta la distribución del espacio y, sobre todo, anteponiendo el respeto por la naturaleza. Entre las últimas apuestas están las luces tenues y las luminarias solares y con ledes. Al distribuir los puntos de luz, hay que decidir el uso que se le dará a cada zona. Para conseguir una luz cenital adecuada en los porches o en las glorietas se pude optar por lámparas de techo o alumbrado descendente con farolas o apliques altos.

Para completar el ambiente en el jardín cabe la posibilidad de incorporar pequeños detalles decorativos que aportarán encanto y ayudarán a personalizar el espacio exterior. El tipo de accesorios dependerá del estilo que se desee y de la composición que se haya logrado después de haber elegido las plantas y haber planificado la forma de los senderos y zonas de piedra.

Se puede optar por macetas decorativas, globos fijos de piedra, estatuas o fuentes, entre muchas otras opciones. Si lo que se busca es un aire más rural, las bañeras para pájaros o pajareras son ideales. También se pueden situar figuras o motivos decorativos sobre las piedras para atraer a mariposas y colibríes. Todos los accesorios harán del jardín un espacio adaptado al gusto personal y aportarán el acabado final a ese rincón agreste de la casa.

Several companies present collections of pieces ideal for the garden consisting of sun loungers, tables, couches, chairs, low chairs, sofas, high tables, footstools, benches or stools.

Verschillende bedrijven presenteren collecties van ideale tuinartikelen, bestaande uit veranda's, tafels, banken, stoelen, fauteuils, sofa's, hoge tafels, voetenbankjes, banken of krukjes.

Zahlreiche Firmen stellen für den Garten gedachte Kollektionen vor, die Sonnenliegen, Tische, Sofas, Stühle, Schemel, hohe Tische, Fußbänke, Bänke und Hocker umfassen.

Numerose ditte presentano nelle loro collezioni composizioni di elementi pensati per il giardino, composte da lettini e sedie sdraio, sedie, poltroncine, divani modulari, tavolini, pouf, panche e sgabelli.

De nombreuses griffes proposent dans leurs collections des ensembles de pièces idéales pour le jardin : transats, tables, chaises, fauteuils bas, canapés modulables, tables hautes, poufs, bancs ou tabourets.

Numerosas firmas presentan en sus colecciones conjuntos de piezas ideales para el jardín compuestos por tumbonas, mesas tumbona, sillas, sillones bajos, sofás modulares, mesas altas, pufs, bancos o taburetes.

Kettal

The Maia collection, designed by Patricia Urquiola, is a light collection which oozes nature. Together the braided design and strength of the aluminum structure fill your outdoor space with vitality.

De Maia collectie, ontworpen door Patricia Urquiola, is een lichte collectie die de natuur naar binnen haalt. Zowel het gevlochten ontwerp als sterke aluminium structuur vult de buitenruimte met levendigheid.

Die von Patricia Urquiola entworfene Maia-Kollektion besticht durch Leichtigkeit und Natürlichkeit. Das Flechtdesign und die robuste Aluminiumstruktur verleihen unseren Räumen im Freien Lebendigkeit.

Maia (design di Patricia Urquiola) è una collezione leggera, nella quale domina la naturalezza delle forme. Il design intrecciato e la solidità della struttura in alluminio creano una combinazione che trasmette energia allo spazio circostante.

La collection Maia, conçue par Patricia Urquiola, est un ensemble léger dominé par le naturel. Le design entrelacé et la solidité de la structure en aluminium créent une combinaison qui remplit l'espace extérieur d'énergie.

La colección Maia, con diseño de Patricia Urquiola, es un conjunto de muebles ligeros en los que prima la naturalidad. El diseño trenzado y la solidez de la estructura de aluminio crean una combinación que llena de energía el espacio exterior.

Inspired by modern architectural forms, this collection makes the nature of the environment stand out. The collection consists of a pergola, fully configurable daybeds and customizable aluminum furniture that fit perfectly into the natural environment.

Von der modernen Architektur inspiriert betont diese Kollektion die Natur der Umgebung. Die Kollektion besteht aus einer Pergola, frei gestaltbaren Liegen und anpassbaren Aluminium-Möbeln, die sich perfekt in die natürliche Umgebung einfügen.

Inspirée des formes architecturales modernes, cette collection met en valeur la nature du milieu environnant. L'ensemble est composé d'une pergola, de lits de jardin entièrement configurables et de meubles en aluminium personnalisables qui s'intègrent à la perfection à l'environnement naturel.

Dankzij deze op moderne architectonische vormen gebaseerde collectie komt de natuurlijke omgeving beter tot zijn recht. De collectie bestaat uit een pergola, een geheel configureerbare zit/slaapbank en gepersonaliseerd aluminium meubilair dat perfect past in de natuurlijke omgeving.

Ispirata a forme architettoniche moderne, questa collezione esalta la natura che la circonda; si compone della pergola, delle *daybeds* completamente configurabile secondo i propri gusti, e di mobili di alluminio personalizzabili che si inseriscono perfettamente nell'ambiente naturale.

Inspirada en formas arquitectónicas modernas, esta colección resalta la naturaleza del entorno. La colección se compone de pérgola, *daybeds* totalmente configurables y muebles de aluminio personalizables que se integran perfectamente en el entorno natural.

Kettal

Daybeds sunloungers are designed to provide an atmosphere of relaxation and tranquility in your outdoor space. They are available in a variety of colors that can be combined with fabrics and aluminum panels.

Zit/slaapbanken zijn ontworpen om een sfeer van ontspanning en rust in uw tuin te creëren. Ze zijn verkrijgbaar in verschillende kleuren, die gecombineerd kunnen worden met stoffen en aluminium panelen.

Liegestühle und Gartenliegen werden entworfen, um eine Atmosphäre der Ruhe und Erholung im Freien zu schaffen. Sie sind in vielen Farben erhältlich, die man mit Stoffen und Aluminium-Elementen kombinieren kann.

I lettini Daybed sono pensati per offrire un ambiente in cui rilassarsi in tutta tranquillità nel proprio spazio esterno. Sono disponibili in una varietà di colorazioni che possono essere combinate con vari tessuti e pannelli di alluminio.

Les lits de jardin sont conçus pour conférer une atmosphère de relaxation et de tranquillité dans votre espace extérieur. Ils sont disponibles dans une grande variété de coloris combinables à une large gamme de tissus et de panneaux en aluminium.

Las tumbonas Daybeds están pensadas para proporcionar un ambiente de relajación y tranquilidad en tu espacio exterior. Están disponibles en una variedad de colores que se pueden combinar con tejidos y paneles de aluminio.

Kettal

This collection of furniture is made from aluminum painted with polyester powder. The modern structures are mobile and provide a relaxing space in any outdoor environment.

Diese Möbelkollektion besteht aus mit Polyesterpulver beschichtetem Aluminium. Die mobilen modernen Strukturen schaffen einen Ruheraum in jeder Outdoor-Umgebung.

Cette collection de mobilier est fabriquée en aluminium peint à base de poudre de polyester. Ses structures modernes sont mobiles et fournissent un espace de détente dans n'importe quel environnement.

Deze meubelcollectie is gemaakt van aluminium en gelakt met polyesterpoeder. De moderne structuren zijn verplaatsbaar en zorgen voor een ontspanningsruimte voor exterieurs.

Questa collezione di arredamento in alluminio verniciato a polveri di poliesteri. Le sue strutture moderne sono mobili e offrono uno spazio di relax a qualsiasi ambiente esterno.

Esta colección de mobiliario es de aluminio pintado con polvo de poliéster. Sus modernas estructuras son móviles y proporcionan un espacio de relax en cualquier ambiente externo.

Kettal

In modern environments metal structures and straight lines are mostly used.

In modernen Umgebungen werden meist Metallstrukturen und gerade Linien bevorzugt.

Dans les atmosphères modernes, les structures métalliques et rectilignes sont prédominantes.

In moderne ambiances worden metalen structuren en rechte lijnen het meest gebruikt.

Negli ambienti moderni predominano le strutture metalliche e dalle linee rette.

En ambientes modernos predominan las estructuras metálicas y de líneas rectas.

Kettal

Kettal

Kettal

Lamps are great for outdoor living areas. In the porch or dining room, this lighting will make green spaces more personal and intimate and provide warmth during summer nights.

Lampen zijn geweldig voor buitenruimtes. In de veranda of eetkamer zorgt deze verlichting voor persoonlijkere en intiemere groene ruimtes en voor een gezellige sfeer tijdens zomeravonden.

Lampen sind großartig für Wohnbereiche im Freien. Auf der Veranda oder im Essbereich macht diese Beleuchtung begrünte Zonen persönlicher und intimer und sorgt in Sommernächten für eine warme Atmosphäre.

Le lampade a piantana sono molto utili per le zone giorno esterne. Nel portico o vicino al tavolo da pranzo, questo tipo di illuminazione permetterà di rendere più personali e intimi gli spazi verdi e più accogliente l'ambiente all'aria aperta nelle notti d'estate.

Les lampes à pied sont très utiles pour les espaces de vie extérieurs. Sous un porche ou dans le coin destiné au repas, ce type d'éclairage permettra de les rendre plus personnels et intimes, tout en conférant de la chaleur à la zone extérieure pendant les nuits d'été.

Las lámparas de pie son muy útiles para las zonas de estar exteriores. En el porche o en el comedor, este tipo de iluminación tranformará los espacios verdes y al aire libre en lugares más personales, íntimos y cálidos, ideales para las noches estivales.

Marset
(left)

Arborètum
Barcelona, Spain
(right)

Marset
(opposite page)

This collection of tables, chairs and flowerpots illuminated with LED lights is an excellent choice for our terrace. With this set of garden furniture you will not need lighting because it is integrated into the furniture. In addition, the flowerpot has a built-in drip irrigation system.

Diese Kollektion von Tischen, Stühlen und beleuchteten LED-Blumentöpfen ist eine ausgezeichnete Wahl für Terrassen. Mit diesem Gartenmöbel-Set braucht man keine Beleuchtung, da diese in die Möbel integriert ist. Zusätzlich hat der Blumentopf ein eingebautes Tropf-Bewässerungssystem.

Cet ensemble composé d'une table, de chaises et de pots éclairés au moyen de diodes est une excellente option pour notre terrasse. Avec ce kit pour jardin vous n'aurez besoin d'aucun éclairage d'appoint car celui-ci est intégré au mobilier. En outre, le pot est pourvu d'un système d'arrosage au goutte à goutte intégré.

Deze collectie tafels, stoelen en verlichte LED-bloempotten is een uitstekende keuze voor uw terras. Met deze tuinmeubelset is verlichting niet nodig, omdat die geïntegreerd is in het meubilair. De bloempot heeft bovendien een ingebouwd druppelbevloeiingsysteem.

Questa collezione con tavolo, sedie e vaso illuminati con LED è un'ottima scelta per la terrazza. Con questo set da giardino non avrete bisogno di altri tipi di illuminazione, dato che quest'ultima è integrata nell'arredamento. Il vaso inoltre dispone di un sistema di irrigazione a goccia incorporato.

Esta colección de mesa, sillas y macetas iluminadas con ledes es una excelente opción para nuestra terraza. Con este juego de jardín no necesitarás iluminación extra, puesto que está integrada en el mobiliario. Además, la maceta lleva incorporado un sistema de riego por goteo.

Arborètum
Barcelona, Spain

Gandía Blasco
(left)

Maset
(right)

Gandía Blasco
(opposite page)

The strength of the forms, the richness of the materials and energy of the fire are the main elements that characterize the ZigZag Collection for Kettal designed by Emiliana Design Studio. Porcelain oil lamps and tables that convert into grills stand out in the collection.

Strenge Formen, Materialreichtum und die Energie des Feuers sind die bezeichnenden Elemente der ZigZag-Kollektion, die das Emiliana Design Studio für Ketta entworfen hat. Öllampen aus Porzellan und Tische, die sich in Grillroste verwandeln, fallen in der Kollektion auf.

La force des formes, la richesse des matériaux et l'énergie du feu sont les principaux éléments qui caractérisent la collection des objets ZigZag de Kettal conçue par Emiliana Design Studio. Il convient de citer les lampes à huile en porcelaine et les tables convertibles en barbecue.

De robuuste vormen, rijkheid van de materialen en de energie van vuur zijn de belangrijkste elementen die de ZigZag Collectie voor Kettal, ontworpen door de Emiliana Design Studio karakteriseren. Opvallend zijn de porseleinen olielampen en de tafels die kunnen worden omgebouwd tot grills.

L'energia delle forme, la ricchezza dei materiali e la potenza del fuoco sono le principali caratteristiche della collezione di oggetti ZigZag di Kettal, progettata da Emiliana Design Studio. Spiccano le lampade a olio di porcellana e i tavoli trasformabili in barbecue.

La fuerza de las formas, la riqueza de los materiales y la energía del fuego son los principales elementos que caracterizan la colección de objetos ZigZag de Kettal diseñada por Emiliana Design Studio. Destacan las lámparas de aceite de porcelana y las mesas convertibles en barbacoa.

Kettal

337

Santa & Cole
(left)

Marset
(right)

Santa & Cole
(opposite page)

A well-lit garden will allow you to appreciate its beauty all the time from inside the house. Exterior wall sconces such as Nagy by Marset are ideal to highlight the entrance.

Een goed verlichte tuin maakt het mogelijk om binnenshuis van al zijn schoonheid te genieten. Lampen aan de buitenmuren, zoals Nagy by Marset, zijn ideaal om de ingang goed te doen uitkomen.

Mit einem gut beleuchteten Garten können Sie dessen Schönheit jederzeit vom Haus aus genießen. Außenwandleuchten wie Nagy von Marset sind ideal für den Eingang.

Un giardino ben illuminato vi permetterà di apprezzare la sua bellezza in ogni momento anche dall'interno della casa. Le applique da parete per esterni, come Nagy di Marset, sono ideali per definire il percorso d'ingresso.

Un jardin bien éclairé nous permettra d'apprécier sa beauté en permanence depuis l'intérieur de la maison. Les appliques murales extérieures comme Nagy de Marset sont idéales pour repérer le chemin d'entrée.

Un jardín bien iluminado nos permitirá apreciar su belleza en todo momento desde el interior de la casa. Los apliques de pared exterior como Nagy de Marset son ideales para marcar el recorrido de entrada.

Flowerpots are also an embellishment for the garden. There are a variety of shapes, colors and materials: clay, terra cotta, plastic or resin, wood, stone or concrete. You should choose them depending on the plant and climatic conditions of the area.

Bloempotten zijn ook een verfraaiing voor de tuin. Ze hebben een scala aan vormen, kleuren en materialen: klei, terracotta, plastic of hars, hout, steen of beton. Houd bij de keuze voor de plant rekening met het klimaat van het gebied.

Blumentöpfe bedeuten auch eine Verschönerung für den Garten. Es gibt sie in allen Formen, Farben und Materialien: Ton, Terrakotta, Kunststoff, Harz, Holz, Stein oder Beton. Man sollte sie der Pflanze und den klimatischen Bedingungen der Gegend entsprechend auswählen.

I vasi sono anche elementi decorativi del giardino. Ne esistono di molteplici forme, colori e materiali: di fango, terracotta, plastica o resina, legno, pietra o calcestruzzo. Si dovrebbero scegliere in funzione della pianta e delle condizioni climatiche dell'ambiente.

Les pots sont également des éléments décoratifs du jardin. Il en existe une grande variété de formes, de couleurs et de matériaux : en argile, en terre cuite, en plastique ou en résine, en bois, en pierre ou en béton. Ils doivent être choisis en fonction de la plante et des conditions climatiques du terrain.

Las macetas también son un elemento decorativo del jardín. Existen una variedad de formas, colores y materiales: de barro, terracota, plástico o resina, madera, piedra u hormigón. Deberían escogerse en función de la planta y las condiciones climáticas del terreno.

Casamania

Galeria Joan Gaspar
(opposite page)

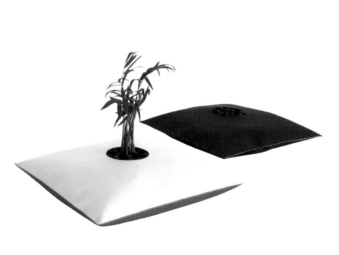

Vondom

Kettal
(opposite page)

Vitamin
(left)

Quoi
(right)

Gandía Blasco
(opposite page)

To enjoy the summer protected in the shade, Gandía Blasco presents the Ensombra sunshade made from stainless steel and formica strips that can be fitted depending on the position of the sun or they can be removed. Another solution that the company offers to escape the sun is the Tipi wigwam with a front door.

Om lekker in de schaduw van de zomer te genieten presenteert Gandía Blasco het Ensombra zonnescherm, gemaakt van roestvrij staal en formica stroken die kunnen worden afgesteld aan de stand van de zon, of kunnen worden verwijderd. Een andere oplossing voor zonwering van bedrijf is de Tipi wigwam met een voordeur, voor een heel bijzonder plekje in uw tuin.

Damit man den Sommer im Schatten genießen kann, stellt Gandía Blasco den Ensombra-Sonnenschirm aus rostfreiem Stahl und Formica-Lamellen vor, die dem Sonnenstand entsprechend angepasst und ineinander geschoben werden können. Eine weitere Lösung, die die Firma anbietet, um sich vor der Sonne zu schützen, ist der Tipi-Wigwam mit einer Vordertür.

Per godersi l'estate all'ombra, Gandía Blasco presenta il parasole Ensombra, fabbricato in ferro termolaccato e con tiranti che possono essere posizionati nel modo voluto o anche tolti. Una delle altre soluzioni per ripararsi dal sole è la tenda indiana Tipi, con entrata frontale.

Pour profiter de l'été à l'ombre, Gandía Blasco présente le parasol Ensombra fabriqué en acier inoxydable et pourvu de planches en formica qui peuvent être déplacées, voire retirées en fonction de la position du soleil. Cette marque propose une autre solution contre les rayons du soleil: le Tipi indien à accès par l'avant.

Para poder disfrutar del verano a la sombra, Gandía Blasco propone el parasol Ensombra. Está fabricado en acero inoxidable y dispone de listones de formica que pueden ajustarse en función de la posición del sol o incluso quitarse. Otra de las soluciones que presenta la firma para protegerse del sol es la tienda india Tipi, con puerta frontal.

Vitamin

Gandía Blasco
(opposite page)

PUBLIC GARDEN

ÖFFENTLICHER GARTEN

JARDIN PUBLIC

OPENBARE TUINEN

GIARDINO PUBBLICO

JARDÍN PÚBLICO

Ecocities: green spaces for urban biodiversity

Ökostädte: grüne Bereiche für die biologische
Vielfalt in der Stadt

Éco-villes : des espaces verts
pour une biodiversité urbaine

Ecocities: groene ruimtes voor
stedelijke biodiversiteit

Eco-città: spazi verdi per la biodiversità urbana

Ecociudades: espacios verdes
para la biodiversidad urbana

Cities have evolved along with humanity and the need for sustainable development is already an undeniable fact. In places like Asia, economic growth and population cause urban concentration, that, for property reasons and speculative use of the land, is leading to true megalopolis. This new urban concept means that green architecture is facing a real challenge and it seems that those involved in new urban planning processes follow the same concepts and advance with the same goal. To achieve eco-efficient cities in terms of water consumption, electricity and other resources. Saving energy in the construction and subsequent maintenance of houses, smart water and electricity grids with the use of active systems, such as solar panels, are only a few technology solutions can be applied.

Several projects have been planned to achieve an urban plan that promotes the biodiversity of cities. Some proposals start from scratch, with real visionary ideas. Others respect the built cities redefining the urban plans. They emphasize the importance of efficient mobility systems to make the city more pleasant and environmentally friendly.

The megalopolises grow vertically making a projection based on bioclimatic architecture necessary: multi-residential dwellings that make use of the energy supplied by the environment to imitate as closely as possible the desired environmental comfort conditions. The arrangement of the windows, the orientation, materials, insulation are a few of the passive strategies applied in these living spaces, sometimes combined with other active strategies. Concepts that are being transferred to the urban plan to achieve sustainable development and self-sufficiency in our cities.

Les villes on évolué au rythme de l'humanité et la nécessité d'un développement durable est aujourd'hui un fait indéniable. Dans certaines parties du monde comme l'Asie, la croissance économique et démographique engendre une concentration urbaine qui, pour des raisons de propriété et d'usage spéculatif du terrain, donne actuellement naissance à de véritables mégapoles. Avec ce nouveau concept urbanistique l'architecture verte se retrouve confrontée à un véritable défi, et il semble que les acteurs des nouveaux processus de planification urbaine suivent tous les mêmes principes et avancent dans une seule et même direction : créer des villes éco-efficaces en termes de consommation d'eau, d'électricité et d'autres ressources. L'économie d'énergie dans la construction et dans l'entretien conséquent des logements, les réseaux intelligents d'approvisionnement en eau et en électricité avec l'utilisation de systèmes actifs, tels que les panneaux solaires, ne sont qu'une partie de la technologie potentielle.

De nombreux projets ont été mis en œuvre pour obtenir un plan d'urbanisme favorisant la biodiversité des grandes villes. Certaines propositions partent de zéro et sont de véritables paris sur l'avenir. D'autres respectent les villes construites en redéfinissant les plans d'urbanisme. L'accent est notamment mis sur des systèmes de mobilité efficaces afin de convertir les villes en des espaces plus agréables et respectueux de l'environnement.

Les mégalopoles grandissent sur le plan vertical, avec la nécessité d'un rayonnement reposant sur l'architecture bioclimatique : des logements multi-résidentiels qui exploitent l'utilisation de l'énergie fournie par l'environnement pour s'approcher le plus possible des conditions de confort environnemental souhaitées. La disposition des fenêtres, l'orientation, les matériaux et l'isolation figurent parmi stratégies passives de ces espaces habitables, qui peuvent parfois être combinées à d'autres stratégies actives. Ces concepts sont intégrés au plan d'urbanisme dans le but de parvenir à un développement durable et autosuffisant de nos villes.

Die Städte haben sich zusammen mit der Menschheit fortentwickelt und die Notwendigkeit einer nachhaltigen Entwicklung ist heute eine unleugbare Tatsache. Durch das wirtschaftliche und demografische Wachstum entstehen z.B. in Asien städtische Ballungsräume, die wegen Eigentums- und Bodenspekulationen zu wahren Mega-Städten werden. Diese neue Entwicklung führt dazu, dass die grüne Architektur einer echten Herausforderung gegenübersteht und es scheint, dass die an den neuen Stadtplanungsverfahren beteiligten Personen den gleichen Konzepten folgen und in einer einzigen Richtung fortschreiten: Ökoeffiziente Städte in Bezug auf Wasserverbrauch, Elektrizität und weitere Ressourcen. Energieersparnis beim Bauen und die konsequente Wartung der Wohnungen sowie intelligente Versorgungsnetze für Wasser und Elektrizität unter Verwendung von aktiven Systemen wie Sonnenkollektoren sind nur ein Teil der Technologie, die angewandt werden kann.

Es wurden zahlreiche Projekte für eine Stadtplanung entworfen, die die biologische Vielfalt der Städte fördert. Einige Vorschläge fangen bei Null an und stellen echte Zukunftsvisionen dar. Andere berücksichtigen die bereits bestehenden Städte und definieren die Stadtentwicklungspläne neu. Sie legen Wert auf effiziente Verkehrssysteme, um aus den Städten angenehmere und umweltfreundlichere Räume zu machen.

Die Megastädte wachsen in die Höhe, wodurch eine Planung, die auf einer bioklimatischen Architektur beruht, notwendig wird: Wohnblocks, die erneuerbare Energien nutzen, um so weit wie möglich den gewünschten Komfort zu bieten. Anordnung der Fenster, Himmelsrichtung, Materialien und Isolierung sind einige der passiven Strategien zur Energieersparnis in diesen Wohnräumen, die gelegentlich mit weiteren aktiven Strategien verbunden werden... Konzepte, die in die Stadtplanung eingehen, um eine nachhaltige und autarke Entwicklung zu erzielen.

Steden hebben zich samen met de mensheid ontwikkeld en de noodzaak voor duurzame ontwikkeling is een feit waar we niet meer omheen kunnen. In gebieden zoals Azië veroorzaakt economische en demografische groei een stedelijke concentratie waardoor er, vanwege eigendom en speculatief gebruik van de grond, heuse metropolen ontstaan. Door dit nieuwe stedelijke concept staat de architectuur voor een uitdaging. Het lijkt erop dat de betrokkenen bij de nieuwe processen van ruimtelijke inrichting nieuwe concepten volgen en deze in een bepaalde richting voortzetten. Doelstelling is het stichten van eco-efficiënte steden voor wat betreft het verbruik van water, elektriciteit en andere hulpbronnen. Energiebesparing in de bouw, een consequent onderhoud van de woningen en intelligente water- en elektriciteitsvoorzieningen door het gebruik van actieve systemen zoals zonnepanelen, vormen slechts een onderdeel van de toepasbare techniek.

Talrijke projecten zijn naar voren gebracht om een stadsplan te ontwikkelen waarin de biodiversiteit van de grote stad wordt bevorderd. Enkele voorstellen beginnen bij nul en zijn daarmee heuse visionaire uitdagingen. Andere gaan uit van de reeds gebouwde steden en stellen een nieuwe definitie van de ruimtelijke inrichting voor. Er wordt belang gehecht aan efficiënte mobiliteitssystemen om de steden aangenamer en milieuvriendelijker te maken.

Metropolen groeien verticale. Projectontwikkeling gebaseerd op bioklimatische architectuur is daarom nodig. In multiresidentiële woningen wordt gebruik gemaakt van door het milieu geleverde energie, voor een zo goed mogelijke aanpassing aan de gewenste eisen van comfort. De plaats van de ramen, ligging, materialen en isolatie zijn enkele passieve strategieën, die soms worden gecombineerd met actieve strategieën. Deze concepten zijn naar stedelijk niveau verheven, om een duurzame en zelfvoorzienende ontwikkeling in onze steden mogelijk te maken.

L'evoluzione delle città è andata di pari passo con l'evoluzione umana, e la necessità di sviluppo sostenibile è oggigiorno un fatto innegabile. Nel continente asiatico la crescita economica e demografica ha originato concentrazioni urbane che, per motivi di proprietà, ed in seguito ad usi speculativi del terreno, stanno dando vita a vere e proprie megalopoli. Questo nuovo concetto urbanistico fa sì che l'architettura verde debba affrontare una vera e propria sfida e pare che le persone coinvolte nei nuovi processi di pianificazione urbana seguano gli stessi concetti ed avanzino in un'unica direzione: creare città eco-efficienti in quanto a consumo idrico, elettrico ed altre risorse. Il risparmio energetico nella costruzione e la conseguente manutenzione delle abitazioni, le reti intelligenti di rifornimento idrico ed elettrico con l'uso di sistemi attivi, come i pannelli solari, sono soltanto una parte della tecnologia applicabile.

Sono stati proposti numerosi progetti per riuscire a creare un piano urbanistico in grado di favorire la biodiversità delle città. Alcune proposte partono da zero e possono essere definite delle autentiche proposte visionarie, altre, invece rispettano le città costruite definendo nuovamente i piani urbanistici. Si dà importanza ai sistemi di mobilità efficienti per fare delle città degli spazi più piacevoli e rispettosi dell'ambiente.

Le megalopoli crescono a livello verticale ed è necessaria una proiezione basata sull'architettura bioclimatica: abitazioni multi-residenziali che sfruttano l'uso dell'energia fornita dall'ambiente per avvicinarsi il più possibile alle condizioni di comfort ambientale desiderate. La disposizione delle finestre, la loro orientazione, i materiali e l'isolamento, sono alcune delle strategie passive di questi spazi abitabili, occasionalmente abbinate ad altre strategie attive. Concetti che si stanno portando sul piano urbanistico per ottenere uno sviluppo sostenibile ed autosufficiente delle nostre città.

Las ciudades han evolucionado junto con la humanidad, y la necesidad para el desarrollo sostenible es ya un hecho innegable. En lugares como en Asia, el crecimiento económico y el demográfico causan una concentración urbana que, por razones de propiedad y uso especulativo del terreno, está dando lugar a verdaderas megalópolis. Esto hace que la arquitectura verde afronte un verdadero reto y parece que los involucrados en los nuevos procesos de planificación urbana siguen los mismos conceptos y avanzan en una sola dirección: conseguir ciudades ecoeficientes en consumo de agua, electricidad y otros recursos. El ahorro de energía en la construcción y el consecuente mantenimiento de las viviendas, las redes inteligentes de abastecimiento de agua y electricidad con la utilización de sistemas activos, como los paneles solares, son sólo una parte de la tecnología que se puede aplicar.

Se han planteado numerosos proyectos para conseguir desarrollos urbanísticos que favorezcan la biodiversidad de las urbes. Algunas propuestas parten de cero, siendo auténticas apuestas visionarias. Otras respetan las ciudades construidas redefiniendo los planes urbanísticos. Se da importancia a los sistemas de movilidad eficientes para hacer de las ciudades espacios más agradables y respetuosos con el medio ambiente.

Las megalópolis crecen en vertical, y es necesaria una proyección basada en la arquitectura bioclimática: viviendas multiresidenciales que aprovechan el uso de la energía abastecida por la naturaleza para acercarse lo más posible a las condiciones de confort ambiental deseadas. La disposición de las ventanas, la orientación, los materiales o el aislamiento son algunas de las estrategias pasivas empleadas en estos espacios habitables, combinadas en ocasiones con estrategias activas. Estos conceptos se están integrando en el plan urbanístico para conseguir el desarrollo sostenible y autosuficiente de nuestras ciudades.

The linear, compact urban development winds its way through the hills. By taking advantage of various different heights, each apartment enjoys a beautiful view of the city.

De lineaire en compacte stadsontwikkeling kronkelt door de heuvels. Door gebruik te maken van de verschillende hoogtes heeft elk appartement een prachtig uitzicht over de stad.

Die kompakte lineare urbane Anlage windet sich über die Hügel. Durch die Ausnutzung der verschiedenen Höhen hat jede Wohnung einen schönen Blick über die Stadt.

Lo sviluppo urbano lineare e compatto si snoda lungo le colline. Sfruttando le varie altezze, ogni appartamento gode di una piacevole vista sulla città.

Le développement urbain linéaire et compact serpente au milieu des collines. Répartis à différentes altitudes, les appartements bénéficient tous d'une jolie vue sur la ville.

El desarrollo urbano lineal y compacto serpentea por las colinas. Al aprovechar las diferentes alturas, cada apartamento tiene una hermosa vista sobre la ciudad.

MVRDV
Logroño, Spain

Schønherr Landskab, Adept Architects
Helsingborg, Sweden

Schønherr Landskab, Adept Architects
Helsingborg, Sweden

The proximity to water in Helsingborg, sustainability, meeting spaces and diversity have been the basic requirements that have marked the project's structure.

De nabijheid van het water van Helsingborg, de duurzaamheid, de vergaderingsruimten en de diversiteit waren de basisvereisten die de opbouw van het project hebben bepaald.

Die Nähe zum Wasser in Helsingborg, Nachhaltigkeit, Orte der Begegnung und Vielfalt sind die grundlegenden Bedingungen, die die Struktur des Projekts ausmachen.

La vicinanza all'acqua di Helsingborg, la sostenibilità, gli spazi comuni e la diversità sono stati i requisiti di base che hanno contraddistinto la struttura del progetto.

À Helsinborg, la proximité de l'eau, la durabilité, les espaces de réunion et la diversité ont été les conditions de base caractéristiques de la structure du projet.

La proximidad al agua de Helsingborg, la sostenibilidad, los espacios de reunión y la diversidad han sido los requisitos básicos que han marcado la estructura del proyecto.

MVRDV
Almere, The Netherlands

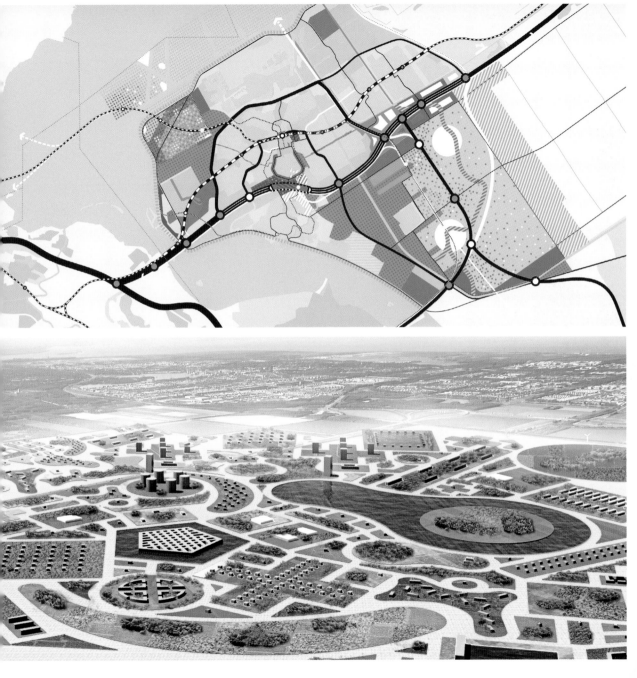

MVRDV
Almere, The Netherlands

The expansion will be distributed in four areas: the island Almere IJland, Almere Pampus, Almere Centre and Oosterworld, an area for the rural and organic city planning.

Het gebouw is in vier zones opgedeeld: Almere IJland, Almere Pampus, Almere Centre en Oosterworld, een zone bestemd voor het meest landelijke en organische urbanisme.

Die Erweiterung ist in vier Zonen aufgeteilt: Die Insel Almere IJland, Almere Pampus, Almere Centre und Oosterworld, ein Bereich der für einen ländlicheren und organischen Städtebau bestimmt ist.

L'ampliamento sarà distribuito in quattro zone: l'isola Almere IJland, Almere Pampus, Almere Centre e Oosterworld, una zona destinata a un urbanismo più rurale e biologico.

L'extension sera répartie en quatre zones : l'île Almere IJland, Almere Pampus, Almere Centre y Oosterworld, une zone consacrée à un urbanisme plus rural et écologique.

La ampliación se distribuirá en cuatro zonas: la isla Almere IJland, Almere Pampus, Almere Centre y Oosterworld, una zona destinada al urbanismo más rural y orgánico.

Cinemas, restaurants and stores are spread across this axis, near the port.

Kinos, Restaurants und Läden erstrecken sich entlang der Ost-Achse neben dem Hafen.

Les cinémas, restaurants et boutiques longent l'axe est, le long du port.

De bioscopen, restaurants en winkels strekken zich langs de oostas, naast de haven, uit.

Cinema, ristoranti e negozi si snodano lungo l'asse est, accanto al porto.

Los cines, restaurantes y tiendas se extienden a lo largo del eje este, al lado del puerto.

Foster & Partners
West Kowloon, Hong Kong

Foster & Partners
West Kowloon, Hong Kong

A modern art museum, various theaters and concert halls are located at the end of the western district. The project will strengthen Hong Kong as a cultural destination.

Aan het eind van het Western District zullen zich een museum voor moderne kunst, diverse theaters en concertzalen bevinden. Het project zal Hongkong als culturele bestemming bevestigen.

Am Ende des Westdistrikts werden sich ein Kunstmuseum, verschiedene Theater und Konzerthallen befinden. Das Projekt wird Hongkong als kulturelles Reiseziel festigen.

Alla fine del quartiere ovest sorgeranno un museo di arte moderna, vari teatri e sale per concerti. Il progetto rafforzerà l'immagine di Hong Kong come città di interesse culturale.

Au bout du quartier ouest, se trouvent un musée d'art moderne, des théâtres et des salles de concert. Le projet confirmera Hong Kong dans son rôle de destination culturelle.

Al final del distrito oeste, se situará un museo de arte moderno, distintos teatros y salas de conciertos. El proyecto consolidará Hong Kong como un destino cultural.

The proposal reflects the twenty-first century needs for innovative sustainable city environments with mixed-use neighborhoods for a high quality life.

Het voorstel weerspiegelt het feit dat in de 21ste eeuw innoverende omgevingen in een duurzame stad met gemengde wijken nodig zijn voor een hoge levenskwaliteit.

Der Vorschlag reflektiert die Notwendigkeit des 21. Jahrhunderts, innovative, nachhaltige städtische Räume zu schaffen, mit gemischt genutzten Stadtvierteln für eine hohe Lebensqualität.

La proposta riflette la necessità del XXI secolo di disporre di ambienti innovativi per città sostenibili con quartieri di uso misto volti a garantire una buona qualità della vita.

La proposition illustre la nécessité du XXIe de parvenir à des environnements novateurs pour les villes durables avec des quartiers à usage mixte offrant une grande qualité de vie.

La propuesta refleja la necesidad del siglo xxi de crear espacios innovadores para las ciudades sostenibles, con barrios de uso mixto que ofrezcan una alta calidad de vida.

archi5 and archi5prod
Stockholm, Sweden

Luc Schuiten projects are genuine visionary proposals which combine a harmonious vision between the city and the plant world.

Die Projekte von Luc Schuiten sind wahrhaft visionäre Entwürfe, in denen Stadt und Pflanzenwelt harmonisch verbunden werden.

Les projets de Luc Schuiten sont d'authentiques propositions visionnaires qui associent une vision harmonique de la ville et du monde végétal.

De projecten van Luc Schuiten zijn ware visionaire voorstellen waarin een harmonieus beeld tussen de stad en de plantenwereld wordt gecombineerd.

I progetti di Luc Schuiten sono proposte visionarie in cui si propone una visione armonica tra città e mondo vegetale.

Los proyectos de Luc Schuiten son auténticas propuestas visionarias en las cuales se combina una visión armónica entre la ciudad y el mundo vegetal.

Luc Schuiten

TOITS DE BRUXELLES   ANNÉE 2058   *Luc Schuiten*   le 7/04/08

LES TOITS DE BRUXELLES.   ANNÉE 2038   *Luc Schuiten*   le 22.04.2008

tec, ARUP
Hamburg-Harburg Harbor, Germany

The aloe vera shaped structures allow vertical movement and access to the apartments. They house shops, indoor gardens, shops and offices.

De structuren in de vorm van aloë vera maken verticaal verkeer en toegang tot de appartementen mogelijk. Er zijn winkels, binnentuinen, winkels en kantoren gevestigd.

Die Bauwerke in Form der Aloe Vera ermöglichen vertikale Zirkulation und Zugang zu den Appartements. Sie beherbergen Geschäftsräume, Innengärten, Läden und Büros.

Le strutture a forma di aloe vera consentono la circolazione verticale e l'accesso agli appartamenti. Ospitano attività commerciali, giardini interni, negozi e uffici.

Les structures en forme d'Aloe vera permettent la circulation verticale et l'accès aux appartements. Elles sont occupées par des commerces, des jardins intérieurs, des boutiques et des bureaux.

Las estructuras con forma de aloe vera permiten la circulación vertical y el acceso a los apartamentos. Albergan comercios, jardines interiores, tiendas y oficinas.

Desitecture
São Paulo, Brasil

The island provides an independent ecosystem where the flow
of air, water, heat and energy are channeled almost naturally.

Auf der Insel ist ein selbständiges Ökosystem vorgesehen, in dem
die Strömungen von Luft, Wasser, Wärme und Energie auf fast
natürliche Weise kanalisiert werden.

L'île vise un écosystème autonome dans lequel les flux d'air,
d'eau, de chaleur et d'énergie sont canalisés de manière
presque naturelle.

Het eiland is bedacht op een autonoom ecosysteem waar de
lucht-, water-, warmte- en energiestromen op bijna natuurlijke
wijze worden gekanaliseerd.

L'isola dispone di un ecosistema autonomo in cui i flussi di aria,
acqua, calore ed energia sono canalizzati in modo quasi naturale.

La isla contempla un ecosistema autónomo donde los flujos de
aire, agua, calor y energía están canalizados de forma casi natural.

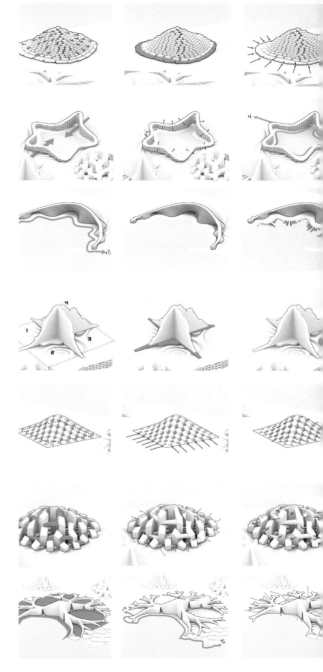

BIG, Bjarke Ingels Group
Zira, Azerbaijan

The landscape architecture is based on the natural landscape of Azerbaijan. It recreates the iconic silhouette of the seven peaks and creates an independent ecosystem.

Het architectonische landschap is gebaseerd op het natuurlijke landschap van Azerbeidzjan. Het herschept de iconische silhouetten van de zeven bergtoppen en creëert een autonoom ecosysteem.

Die Architekturlandschaft basiert auf der natürlichen Landschaft von Aserbaidschan. Sie bildet die Silhouetten der emblematischen sieben Gipfel nach und schafft ein selbständiges Ökosystem.

Il paesaggio architettonico si basa su quello naturale dell'Azerbaigian. Ricrea i profili simbolici delle sette vette e dà vita a un ecosistema autonomo.

Le paysage architectonique est calqué sur le paysage naturel d'Azerbaïdjan. Il recrée les silhouettes icônes des sept sommets et crée un écosystème autonome.

El paisaje arquitectónico se basa en el paisaje natural de Azerbaiyán. Recrea las siluetas icónicas de los siete picos y crea un ecosistema autónomo.

Sweco
Caofeidian, China

Sweco
Caofeidian, China

Caofeidan seeks to achieve climate neutrality, with up to 95% renewable energy. It will have an ecological park that will be open to the public.

De bedoeling van Caofeidan is de klimatische neutraliteit bereiken met tot 95% hernieuwbare energieën. Het zal over een voor het publiek geopend ecologisch park beschikken.

Caofeidan ist so konzipiert, dass die Klimatisierung bis zu 95% mit erneuerbaren Energien erfolgt. Die Anlage verfügt über einen ökologischen Park, der für die Öffentlichkeit zugänglich ist.

Caofeidan è destinata a raggiungere la neutralità climatica con l'uso del 95% di energie rinnovabili. Disporrà di un parco ecologico aperto al pubblico.

Caofeidian a pour but de parvenir à une neutralité climatique, avec 95 % d'énergies renouvelables. Un parc écologique ouvert au public y est prévu.

Caofeidan está destinada a conseguir la neutralidad climática, con hasta un 95% de energías renovables. Contará con un parque ecológico abierto al público.

Green urban areas: parks, squares and avenues

Grüne Stadtgebiete: Parks, Plätze und Straßen

Zones urbaines vertes : parcs, squares et avenues

Groene stedelijke zones: parken, pleinen en avenues

Aree Verdi urbane: parchi, piazza e viali

Áreas verdes urbanas: parques, plazas y avenidas

Landscape architecture, whose name was coined by Gilbert Laing Meason in his *Landscape Architecture of the Great Painters of Italy* (London, 1828), is the discipline that combines the design, planning, management, preservation and rehabilitation of the land. This task allows you to mold and shape the space around the existing architecture or in a developing urban or regional plan. This discipline combines animate objects (plant, tree, water, climate) and inanimate (pavement, surface, furniture), starting from a geographical and social context (urban, suburban and rural) and some technical and economic conditions.

The creation of green spaces in the city, either in the form of parks, squares and avenues, are a response to an established urban development whose objective is environmental protection. Trees help remove pollutants from the air particles such as dust, smoke, pollen or ash. In addition, they eliminate toxic gases, absorbing carbon dioxide and providing oxygen to the atmosphere every day (1,000 cubic meters per day, each tree).

These green spaces also function as urban purifiers, reducing noise pollution from 8 to 10 decibels per meter of thickness of the tree, and they can lower the temperature between 1 and 3 degrees in summer.

A typology needs to be established when designing a green city that involves counting the green spaces that will be required from the point of view of their social function or environmental benefit. With the proper distribution of urban green spaces, taking into account the radii of influence, the needs of its people will be satisfied and a sustainable urban environment will be achieved.

Die Landschaftsarchitektur, die Ihren Namen durch das Werk von Gilbert Laing Meason: *Landscape Architecture of the Great Painters of Italy* (London 1828) erhielt, ist die Disziplin, die Design, Planung, Verwaltung, Erhaltung und Wiederherstellung der Landschaft verbindet. Diese Aufgabe erlaubt es, das Terrain zu formen und den Raum um die bestehende Architektur oder innerhalb einer Stadt- oder Regionalplanung zu gestalten. In dieser Disziplin werden belebte Komponenten (Pflanzen, Bäume, Wasser, Klima) und unbelebte (Bodenbelag, Oberfläche, Mobiliar) vereint, die von einem geographischen und sozialen (städtischen, vorstädtischen und ländlichen) Gefüge und von technischen und wirtschaftlichen Bedingungen ausgehen.

Die Schaffung von städtischen Grünzonen in Form von Parks, Plätzen oder Alleen ist die Reaktion auf eine etablierte Stadtentwicklung. Ihr erklärtes Ziel ist der Umweltschutz. Bäume helfen, kontaminierende Partikel wie Staub, Rauch, Pollen oder Asche aus der Luft zu entfernen. Außerdem eliminieren sie giftige Gase, indem sie Kohlendioxid absorbieren und der Luft täglich Sauerstoff zuführen (1000 Kubikmeter pro Baum).

Diese grünen Räume fungieren nicht nur als Stadtreiniger, sondern reduzieren außerdem die Lärmbelästigung um 8 bis 10 Dezibel pro Meter Baumkrone und können im Sommer die Temperatur bis zu 3 Grad senken.

Für die grüne Planung einer Stadt ist es notwendig, eine Typologie der Grünzonen zu erstellen, die aus der Sicht ihrer sozialen Funktion und ihrer Vorteile für die Umwelt notwendig sind. Mit einer entsprechenden Anordnung der städtischen Grünflächen und unter Berücksichtigung ihres Wirkungskreises werden die Bedürfnisse der Einwohner befriedigt und es wird eine nachhaltige städtische Umwelt erreicht.

L'architecture du paysage, terme utilisé pour la première fois par Gilbert Laing Meason dans son ouvrage *The Landscape Architecture of the Great Painters of Italy* (Londres, 1828), est une discipline alliant design, planification, gestion, préservation et réhabilitation du paysage. Cet art permet de modeler le terrain et l'espace autour de l'architecture existante ou dans le cadre d'un plan d'urbanisme ou régional en développement. Cette discipline repose sur des supports physiques animés (plantes, arbres, eau, climat) et inanimés (revêtement, surface, mobilier), qui partent d'un contexte géographique et social (urbain, périurbain et rural) et certaines conditions techniques et économiques.

La création d'espaces verts dans la ville, que ce soit sous forme de parcs, de places ou d'avenues, est une réponse à un développement urbain établi dont l'objectif réside dans la protection environnementale. Les arbres aident à éliminer les particules polluantes de l'air, comme la poussière, la fumée, le pollen ou les cendres. De plus, ils permettent également d'éliminer les gaz toxiques en absorbant le dioxyde de carbone et en apportant de l'oxygène chaque jour dans l'atmosphère (1 000 mètres carrés par jour, par arbre).

Ces espaces verts, en plus d'agir comme purificateurs urbains, réduisent la nuisance sonore de 8 à 10 décibels par mètre d'épaisseur de la cime de l'arbre, et peuvent parvenir à diminuer la température de 1 à 3 degrés pendant l'été.

Pour la planification verte d'une ville et lors de la comptabilisation des espaces verts prévus, il est nécessaire d'établir une typologie basée sur leur rôle social ou leur apport environnemental. Avec une répartition appropriée des espaces verts urbains, en tenant compte des rayons d'influence, il sera possible de répondre aux besoins des habitants et de créer un environnement urbain durable.

Landschapsarchitectuur, een uitdrukking die voor het eerst gebruikt werd door Gilbert Laing Meason in zijn werk "Landscape Architecture of the Great Painters of Italy" (Londen, 1828), is de discipline die ontwerp, planning, beheer, behoud en renovatie van de grond omvat. Deze taak maakt het mogelijk om het terrein vorm te geven en om de ruimte rond de bestaande architectuur of binnen een stedenbouwkundig of regionaal plan in ontwikkeling te modelleren. Binnen deze discipline worden bezielde elementen (plant, boom, water, klimaat) en onbezielde elementen (plaveisel, oppervlak, meubilair) met elkaar verenigd vanuit een geografische en sociale context (stedelijk, aan de rand van de stad en landelijk) en met inachtneming van technische en economische bepalende factoren.

De inrichting van groenzones in de stad, hetzij in de vorm van parken, pleinen of boulevards, is een reactie op de gevestigde stedelijke ontwikkeling en heeft als doelstelling de bescherming van het milieu. Bomen helpen om vervuilende luchtdeeltjes zoals stof, rook, pollen of as uit de lucht te halen. Ze nemen bovendien schadelijke gassen weg doordat ze dagelijks kooldioxide uit de atmosfeer opnemen en zuurstof afgeven (1.000 kubieke meter per dag per boom).

Naast de functie van stedelijke luchtreinigers verminderen deze groene ruimtes de geluidshinder met 8 tot 10 decibel per meter dikte van de boomkruin, en kunnen ze de temperatuur in de zomer met 1 tot 3 graden verlagen.

Voor de groene inrichting van een stad is het nodig om een indeling vast te stellen bij het bepalen van het aantal groenzones dat nodig is, uitgaande van de sociale functie of van de voordelen voor het milieu. Met een geschikte indeling van de stedelijke groenzones en rekening houdende met de invloedsstraal, kan er worden voldaan aan de behoeften van de inwoners en kan er een duurzame stedelijke omgeving worden gecreëerd.

'architettura del paesaggio, denominazione creata da Gilbert Laing Meason nella sua opera
Landscape Architecture of the Great Painters of Italy (Londra, 1828), è la disciplina che unisce
progettazione, pianificazione, gestione, preservazione e ristrutturazione della terra. Si tratta di un
lavoro che consente di modellare il terreno e lo spazio attorno all'architettura esistente o a piani
urbanistici e regionali in via di sviluppo. In questa disciplina si uniscono supporti fisici animati
(piante, alberi, acqua, clima) ed inanimati (pavimenti, superfici, arredi urbano) che partono da
contesti geografici e sociali (urbano, periurbano e rurale) e fattori condizionanti tecnici
ed economici.
La creazione di spazi verdi all'interno della città, sottoforma di parchi, piazze o viali, sono la
risposta ad uno sviluppo urbanistico prestabilito il cui obiettivo è la protezione ambientale. Gli
alberi aiutano ad eliminare le particelle contaminanti dell'aria, come la polvere, il fumo, il polline
e le ceneri. Eliminano, inoltre, i gas tossici, assorbendo il biossido di carbonio ed apportando
ogni giorno ossigeno all'atmosfera (1.000 metri cubici giornalieri per albero).
Questi spazi verdi, oltre ad essere dei veri e propri purificatori urbani, riducono l'inquinamento
acustico di 8 -10 dB per metro di spessore della cima dell'albero e possono provocare una
riduzione della temperatura pari a 1 - 3 ºC nella stagione estiva.
Per la pianificazione verde di una città sarà necessario stabilire una tipologia nel contabilizzare
gli spazi verdi necessari tenendo conto della loro benefica funzione sociale o ambientale. Grazie
ad un'adeguata distribuzione degli spazi verdi urbani, e tenendo conto del loro raggio d'influenza,
si riuscirà a soddisfare le necessità degli abitanti creando un ambiente urbano sostenibile.

La arquitectura del paisaje, cuya denominación fue acuñada por Gilbert Laing Meason en su
obra *Landscape Architecture of the Great Painters of Italy* (Londres, 1828), es la disciplina que
úna diseño, planificación, gestión, preservación y rehabilitación de la tierra. Esta tarea permite
moldear el terreno y modelar el espacio en torno a la arquitectura existente o en un plan
urbanístico o regional en desarrollo. En esta disciplina se incluyen elementos físicos animados
(planta, árbol, agua, clima) e inanimados (pavimento, superficie, mobiliario), que parten de
un contexto geográfico y social (urbano, periurbano y rural) y unos condicionantes técnicos y
económicos.
La creación de espacios verdes en la ciudad, ya sea en forma de parques, plazas o avenidas,
son la respuesta a un desarrollo urbanístico establecido cuyo objetivo reside en la protección
medioambiental. Los árboles ayudan a reducir las partículas contaminantes del aire, como el
polvo, el humo, el polen o las cenizas. Además, también eliminan los gases tóxicos, absorbiendo
el dióxido de carbono y aportando oxígeno a la atmósfera diariamente (cada árbol aporta hasta
1.000 m³ de oxígeno a la atmósfera al día).
Estos espacios verdes, además de funcionar como purificadores urbanos, reducen la
contaminación sonora entre 8 y 10 decibelios por cada metro de espesor de la copa del árbol,
y pueden lograr disminuir la temperatura entre 1 y 3 grados en verano.
Para la planificación verde de una ciudad será necesario establecer una tipología a la hora de
contabilizar los espacios verdes que se necesitarán desde el punto de vista de su función social
y del beneficio medioambiental. Con una adecuada distribución de los espacios verdes urbanos,
teniendo en cuenta los radios de influencia, se conseguirá satisfacer las necesidades de sus
habitantes y conseguir un entorno urbano sostenible.

In this design, respect for the surroundings was a priority. The platform's cement structure is connected to the terrain by a series of steel tubes drilled into the rock, some as deep as 39 feet into the ground. This plan avoided excavation that might have damaged the roots of the trees.

Bij ontwerpen heeft respect voor de omgeving prioriteit. De betonnen structuur van het platform is aan het terrein verbonden door middel van enkele stalen buizen die in de rotsen zijn geboord, enkele maar liefst 12 meter onder de grond. Deze opzet maakte uitgravingen, waardoor de wortels konden worden beschadigd, overbodig.

Carl-Viggo Hølmebakk
Stor-Elvdal, Norway

Bei diesem Entwurf stand der Schutz der Umgebung an erster Stelle. Die Betonplattform ist durch bis zu zwölf Meter tief verankerte Stahlrohre mit dem Boden verbunden. Dadurch konnten Grabungsarbeiten vermieden werden, die den Baumwurzeln geschadet hätten.

Nel progetto si è data massima priorità al rispetto dell'ambiente. La struttura di calcestruzzo della piattaforma è fissata al terreno per mezzo ditubolari d'acciaio ancorati alla roccia con perforazioni profonde fino a12 m. Questa tecnica ha evitato di dover realizzare scavi che avrebbero danneggiato le radici degli alberi.

Le design met l'accent sur le respect de l'environnement. La structure en béton de la plate-forme est reliée au terrain par des tubes en acier fixés aux rochers, certains jusqu'à 12 m sous terre. Cette option a permis d'éviter des excavations qui auraient pu nuire aux racines des arbres.

En el diseño, el respeto por el entorno ha sido prioritario. La estructura de hormigón de la plataforma se conecta al terreno mediante unos tubulares de acero taladrados a las rocas, algunos hasta 12 m bajo tierra. Este esquema ha evitado excavaciones que dañaran las raíces de los árboles.

The central role of nature in Van de Lindeloof's design allows the cemetery to be a place where peace and serenity invite a desire to stroll and enjoy the aesthetics, in addition to complying with its primordial function. The tombs and crypt walls have a height determined by their function and integrate harmoniously with their surroundings.

De centrale rol van de natuur in het ontwerp van Van de Lindeloof maakt dat de begraafplaats, naast dat het zijn belangrijkste functie vervult, ook een plaats van vrede en rust is, die uitnodigt om te wandelen en de schoonheid te aanschouwen. De grafheuvels en de muren met grafnissen, waarvan de hoogte bepaald is door de functie die ze vervullen, zijn op harmonieuze wijze in de omgeving geïntegreerd.

In Jos van de Lindeloofs Entwurf spielt die Natur die Hauptrolle, was dazu führt, dass der Friedhof nicht nur seine eigentliche Funktion erfüllt, sondern auch ein Ort der Ruhe ist, der zum Spazierengehen einlädt und einen ästhetischen Genuss bietet. Die Grabhügel und -nischen, deren Höhe von ihrer jeweiligen Funktion bestimmt wird, fügen sich harmonisch in die Umgebung ein.

Il ruolo principale della natura nel progetto di Van de Lindeloof fa sì che il cimitero, oltre a soddisfare la sua funzione originaria, sia anche un luogo a cui pace e tranquillità invitano a passeggiare immersi nel godimento estetico. I tumuli e le mura con i loculi, la cui altezza è determinata dalloro funzione, sono armoniosamente integrati nell'ambiente.

Grâce au rôle central joué par la nature dans le design de Van de Lindeloof le cimetière, en plus de remplir sa fonction principal, est également un espace où règnent la paix et le calme, invitant à la promenade et à l'esthétisme. Les tombeaux et les murs, dont la hauteur est définie par leur fonction, s'intègrent harmonieusement dans le paysage.

El papel central que desempeña la naturaleza en el diseño de Van de Lindeloof hace que el cementerio, además de satisfacer su función primordial, sea también un espacio de paz y sosiego que invita al paseo y a la contemplación. Los túmulos y los muros de nichos, cuya altura está determinada por la función que desempeñan, se integran armoniosamente en el entorno.

Jos van de Lindeloof Tuin en Landschapsarchitectenbureau
Zwaanshoek, The Netherlands

Hideki Yoshimatsu & Archipro Architects
Mirasaka, Japan

PWP Landscape Architecture
Saint Louis, MO, USA
(opposite page)

In the central area we find an enclosure wall and building structures that are remains of houses that were never completed. They've made use of these remains by creating a series of footbridges connecting the enclosure wall with the beams and metal or reinforced concrete columns.

In het middengedeelte bevindt zich een muur en de skeletten van gebouwen. Het zijn overblijfselen van een aantal woningen die nooit zijn afgebouwd. Om deze resten opnieuw te gebruiken zijn enkele accesos die de muur verbonden met de balken en de metalen of gewapend betonnen pilaren veranderd in verheven passerelles.

Im zentralen Bereich des Parkgeländes befinden sich eine Mauer und die Gerüste einiger Bauruinen. Stege verbinden die Mauer mit den Balken und Säulen aus Stahl oder Beton.

Nella zona centrale si trovano un muro di recinzione e gli scheletri di edifici che sono i resti di case mai terminate. Per riutilizzarli, gli accessiche uniscono il muro di recinzione alle travi e ai pilastri metallici o di cemento armato, si trasformano in passerelle sopraelevate.

Dans la zone centrale se trouvent un mur de clôture et les ruines d'édifices qui sont les vestiges de maisons dont la construction n'a jamais été achevée. Afin de réutiliser ces restes, des accès reliant le mur aux poutres et aux piliers en métal ou en béton armé ont été transformés en passerelles surélevées.

En la zona central existen un muro de cerramiento y las estructuras de unos edificios que nunca se terminaron. Para reutilizar estos elementos, se construyeron unas pasarelas elevadas que conectan el muro con las vigas y con los pilares metálicos o de hormigón armado.

Rosa Grena Kliass Arquitectura Paisajística
São Paulo, Brasil

EDAW
Manchester, United Kingdom

The Piccadilly Gardens rehabilitation is the first step in a regeneration of the urban center that rectifies an absence of large green spaces in the city. The park also revitalizes a part in the middle that was affected by an IRA bombing. The most dynamic element is the fountain, situated at the garden's center.

De renovatie van de Piccadilly tuinen vormde het uitgangspunt voor het herstel van de binnenstad en voor het compenseren van het gebrek aan grote groenzones. Het park zorgt bovendien voor meer leven in een deel van het centrum waar een bom van de IRA was gevallen. Het meest dynamische element van het geheel is een fontein in het midden van de tuinen.

Die Neugestaltung der Piccadilly Gardens bildete den Ausgangspunkt für die Sanierung des Stadtzentrums und behob den Mangel an großen Grünflächen. Der Park belebt zudem den Teil des Zentrums, der von einer Bombe der IRA verwüstet wurde. Dynamisches Element in der Mitte der Anlage ist ein Granit-Teich mit verspielten Springbrunnen.

La ristrutturazione dei giardini Piccadilly è il punto di partenza per la rinascita del centro urbano e pone rimedio all'assenza di grandi spazi verdi. Il parco dà nuova vita a una parte del centro che era stata colpita da una bomba dell'IRA. L'elemento più dinamico del complesso è la fontana, situata al centro dei giardini.

La rénovation des jardins Piccadilly représente un point de départ pour la transformation du centre urbain et résout le problème de l'absence de grands espaces verts. De plus, le parc redonne de la vitalité à une partie du centre qui avait été détruite par une bombe de l'IRA. L'élément le plus dynamique de l'ensemble est la fontaine située au centre des jardins.

La rehabilitación de los jardines Piccadilly supone un punto de partida para la regeneración del centro urbano y subsana la ausencia de grandes espacios verdes. El parque revitaliza además una parte del centro que fue afectada por una bomba del IRA. El elemento más dinámico del conjunto corresponde a la fuente situada en el centro de los jardines.

Proap
Ourém, Portugal

The emblematic Harz Mountains are the park's natural frame and inspire the different geological and mineral motifs integrated into its design. One example of this is the limestone walls, which evoke the old mine works of the region.

De emblematische heuvels van de Harz vormen het natuurlijke kader van het park en zijn een bron van inspiratie van de verschillende geologische en mijnwerkersmotieven die in het ontwerp zijn geïntegreerd. Een voorbeeld daarvan zijn de kalkstenen muren, die de oude mijnbouw van de regio in herinnering roepen.

Die malerische Kulisse des Harz bildet den natürlichen Rahmen des Parks. Architektonische Elemente wie die Kalksteinwände stellen einen Bezug zur geologischen Beschaffenheit der Umgebung und der Geschichte des Bergbaus her.

Le emblematiche montagne di Harz fanno da cornice naturale al parco e ispirano i diversi motivi geologici e minerari in esso presenti. Ne sono esempio le mura di pietra calcarea, che evocano l'antico sfruttamento minerario della regione.

Les montagnes emblématiques de Harz sont le cadre naturel du parc et inspirent les différents motifs géologiques et minéraux qui composent son design. Les murs en pierre calcaire en sont un bon exemple, évoquant les anciennes exploitations minières de la région.

Las emblemáticas montañas de Harz son el marco natural del parque e inspiran los diferentes motivos geológicos y mineros que integran su diseño. Un ejemplo de ello son los muros de piedra caliza, que evocan las antiguas explotaciones mineras de la región.

Arpas Arquitectos Paisagistas Asociados, Santa-Rita Arquitectos
Beja, Portugal
(left)

Hutterreimann & Cejka Landschaftsarchitekten,
Jens Schmahl/A Lab Architektur
Wernigerode, Germany
(right)

Rosa Grena Kliass Arquitectura Paisajística
São Paulo, Brasil
(opposite page)

In both the most decorative elements and the concept of the park itself, the cubist painting *Horta de Sant Joan* by Picasso inspired the multiple fragmented shapes found in the park's different corners. This influence allowed for the creation of a green area between the various blocks of housing.

Zowel in de meest decoratieve elementen als in de conceptie van het park zelf is het kubistische schilderij *Horta de Sant Joan* van Picasso een bron van inspiratie geweest voor de talrijke gefragmenteerde vormen die we op verschillende plekken in het park aantreffen. Met die inspiratie is een groenzone aangelegd tussen de verschillende bestaande woningblokken.

Sowohl für die dekorativen Elemente, die vielfach zergliederten Formen, die sich in den verschiedenen Bereichen des Parks finden lassen, als auch für das generelle Konzept diente Pablo Picassos Gemälde *Horta de Sant Joan* als Inspiration. Unter diesem Einfluss entstand eine Grünfläche zwischen den vorhandenen Wohnblocks.

Ispirazione delle molteplici forme frammentate presenti nei diversi angoli del parco è stato il quadro cubista *Horta de Sant Joan* di Picasso, sia rispetto agli elementi più decorativi, sia rispetto alla concezione stessa del parco. Questa influenza ha permesso la creazione di un'area verde tra i diversi blocchi di abitazioni esistenti.

Qu'il s'agisse des éléments plus décoratifs ou de la conception même du parc, le tableau cubiste *Horta de Sant Joan* de Picasso a inspiré les multiples formes fragmentées éparpillées aux quatre coins du parc. Cette influence a permis la création d'un espace vert au milieu des blocs de logements existants.

Los cuadros cubistas de Horta de Sant Joan de Picasso inspiraron las múltiples formas fragmentadas que encontramos en distintos rincones del parque, tanto en sus elementos más decorativos como en su diseño. Esta influencia llevó a crear también un área verde entre los varios bloques de viviendas existentes.

Arriola & Fiol Arquitectes
Barcelona, Spain

BB & GG Arquitectes
Barcelona, Spain

Mosbach Paysagistes
Bordeaux, France

In deference to the terrain's marked length, the garden is composed of a series of six thematic spaces through which the visitor can travel by way of established routes separated by environment: a crop, a gallery that reproduces the Aquitaine Basin, a path for the pioneer species of plants, a grove for climbing plants, the aquatic and urban gardens.

Vanwege de opvallende lengte van het perceel bestaat de tuin uit een opeenvolging van zes thematische ruimtes, waardoor de bezoeker zich kan bewegen binnen vastgestelde tracés die in verschillende entourages zijn ingedeeld: bouwland, de galerij die een reproductie van het Aquitaans bekken is, het pad van de pioniersplanten, het populierenbos van klimplanten en water- en stedelijke tuinen.

Um der Längsausdehnung des Grundstücks Rechnung zu tragen, wurde der Garten in sechs aufeinanderfolgende Themengärten unterteilt, die der Besucher über miteinander verknüpfte Spazierwege begehen kann: Ackerbauflächen, eine Nachempfindung des aquitanischen Beckens, den Pfad der Pionierpflanzen, die Allee der Kletterpflanzen, den Wasser- und den Stadtgarten.

A causa della significativa lunghezza dell'appezzamento, il giardino è costituito da una successione di sei spazi tematici, attraverso i quali il visitatore si muove seguendo tracciati stabiliti e separati nei diversi ambienti: l'area delle coltivazioni, la galleria che riproduce la valle aquitana, il sentiero delle piante pioniere, il viale delle piante rampicanti ei giardini acquatici e urbani.

La longueur de la parcelle a été exploitée pour décliner le jardin en une succession de six espaces thématiques parmi lesquels le visiteur peut se promener, et profiter de différentes ambiances, selon un parcours établi : le champs des cultures, la galerie reproduite par le bassin aquitain, le sentier des plantes pionnières, la promenade des plantes grimpantes, les jardins aquatique et urbain.

Debido a la longitud de la parcela, el jardín está compuesto por una sucesión de seis espacios temáticos, a través de los cuales el visitante se mueve en trazados establecidos y separados en ambientes: el campo de los cultivos, la galería que reproduce la cuenca aquitana, el sendero de las plantas pioneras, la alameda de las trepadoras y los jardines acuático y urbano.

Two large sets of stairs grant access to the upper levels of the vertical steel construction, leading visitors to the terrace's vantage point on the top floor. The atrium marked by the structure is used as an open space for leisure and entertainment activities.

Twee brede trappen leiden naar de bovenverdiepingen van de verticale stalen constructie en komen uit op het terras met uitkijkpunt op de bovenste verdieping. Het door de structuur afgebakende voorhof is een open ruimte die bedoeld is voor ludieke en vrijetijdsactiviteiten.

Zwei breite Treppen führen zu den oberen Ebenen der Stahlkonstruktion, zur Aussichtsterrasse auf der obersten Etage. Der Innenhof lädt zum Spielen und Verweilen ein.

Due ampie scale conducono ai livelli superiori della costruzione verticale d'acciaio e terminano sulla terrazza panoramica situata al piano più alto. L'atrio delimitato dalla struttura è uno spazio aperto adatto alle attività ludiche e al riposo.

Deux larges escaliers conduisent aux niveaux supérieurs de la construction verticale en acier et prennent fin à la terrasse-mirador située au plus haut niveau. La cour intérieure, délimitée par la structure, est un espace ouvert qui s'adapte aux activités ludiques et de loisirs.

Dos amplias escaleras conducen hasta los niveles superiores de la construcción vertical edificada en acero y terminan en la terraza-mirador ubicada en la planta más alta. El atrio delimitado por la estructura es un espacio abierto que se adapta a las actividades lúdicas y de ocio.

Burckhardt & Partner Architekten, Raderschall Landschaftsarchitekten
Zurich, Switzerland

Urbanus Architecture & Design
Shenzen, China

Jigsaw puzzle shapes sheathed in brightly-colored mosaic tile, vaguely reminiscent of a swimming pool, make up one of the oasis islands that float in the flowing lines of the brick pavement. The dynamic and chaotic urban environment presses in from all sides of this plaza.

Vormen van puzzelstukjes, opgevuld met mozaïektegels in levendige kleuren die vaag doen denken aan een zwembad, vormen een van de «oase-eilanden» die in de lijnen van het betegelde plaveisel lijken te drijven. De stedelijke, dynamische en chaotische sfeer drukt op alle kanten van het plein.

Formen wie Puzzlestücke in leuchtend bunten Mosaikkacheln, die vage an ein Schwimmbecken erinnern, bilden eine „Oasen-Insel", die auf den fließenden Linien des Ziegelpflasters dahinzutreiben scheint. Die laute und chaotische urbane Umgebung bedrängt den Platz von allen Seiten.

Forme simili a pezzi di un rompicapo incassati in piastrelle a mosaico dai colori vivaci, che ricordano vagamente una piscina, compongono una delle "isole-oasi" che galleggia sul pavimento di mattoni. L'ambiente urbano, dinamico e caotico, preme a ogni lato della piazza.

Des pièces en forme de casse-têtes, recouvertes de carreaux de mosaïques de couleurs vives faisant vaguement penser à une piscine, forment l'une des « îles oasis » flottant sur les lignes du revêtement en briques. L'atmosphère urbaine, dynamique et chaotique, imprègne tous les recoins de cette place.

Piezas en formas de rompecabezas cubiertas de baldosas de mosaico de colores vivos que recuerdan vagamente una piscina componen una de las «islas oasis» que flota en las líneas del pavimento de ladrillo. El ambiente urbano, dinámico y caótico, impregna todos los rincones de esta plaza.

Turenscape
Zhongshan, China

EDAW
Tianjin, China

Made Associati Architettura e Paesaggio
Cendon di Silea, Italy
(opposite page)

The simplicity of the materials chosen for the intervention, like stone, steel, wood and the rustic finish all enable the project's discreet integration into the Sile riverfront. Also integrated into this use of practical materials are a social center, a small square, a church sacristy and a green area.

De eenvoud van de uitgekozen materialen, zoals steen, staal of hout, en de landelijke afwerking zorgen ervoor dat ze op een discrete manier zijn geïntegreerd in de oever van de Sile. Bovendien gaan het ontmoetingscentrum, het pleintje, de sacristie van de kerk en de groenzone perfect samen dankzij het gebruik van deze praktische materialen.

Die Auswahl schlichter Materialien wie Holz, Stahl und Stein sowie ihre rustikale Verarbeitung sorgen für eine unauffällige Einpassung in die Uferlandschaft des Sile. Zudem konnten mithilfe dieser Materialien ein soziales Zentrum, ein kleiner Platz, die Kirchensakristei und eine Grünfläche optisch perfekt einbezogen werden.

La semplicità dei materiali scelti per l'intervento, quali la pietra, l'acciaio eil legno, insieme alla rifinitura rustica, garantiscono l'integrazione discreta con la sponda del fiume Sile. L'uso di questi materiali pratici permette inoltre la perfetta integrazione del centro sociale, della piazzetta, della sagrestia della chiesa e della zona verde.

La simplicité des matériaux choisis pour l'intervention, tels que la pierre, l'acier ou le bois, et leur finition rustique assurent leur intégration discrète sur la rive du Sile. De plus, l'utilisation de matériaux pratiques permet d'intégrer à la perfection le centre social, la petite place, la sacristie de l'église et l'espace vert.

La sencillez de los materiales escogidos en esta intervención, como la piedra, el acero o la madera, así como su acabado rústico, han logrado integrar discretamente el proyecto en la ribera del Sile. Además, el uso de materiales prácticos ha permitido integrar también el centro social, la plazoleta, la sacristía de la iglesia y la zona verde.

Janet Rosenberg & Associate, CS&P Architects
Welland, Canada

Miró Rivera Architects
Austin, TX, USA
(opposite page)

Planted with willows and maple trees, the green hills occupy the majority of the surface area. The wooden path and the bright sunshades planted in the sand beside the water provide the park with a beach-type character that pushes the city into the background.

De met wilgen en esdoorn beplante groene heuvelruggen nemen het grootste deel van het oppervlak in beslag. De houten wandelweg en de opvallende parasols die in de strook zand zijn gestoken, aan de oevers van het water, geven het strandkarakter aan en zorgen ervoor dat de stad op de achtergrond blijft.

Der größte Teil des Geländes besteht aus Grünflächen, die mit Weiden und Ahornbäumen bepflanzt wurden. Der Holzweg und die auffälligen, in den Sand gesetzten gelben Sonnenschirme am Ufer sorgen für Strandatmosphäre und lassen die Stadt in den Hintergrund treten.

Piantate a salici e aceri, le collinette verdi occupano la maggior parte della superficie. Il sentiero di legno e gli ombrelloni vivaci disposti nella fascia sabbiosa accanto all'acqua, sottolineano la sua identità di spiaggia, lasciando la città in secondo piano.

Recouvertes de saules et d'érables, les collines vertes occupent la majeure partie de la superficie. La promenade en bois et les parasols voyants disposés le long de la bande de sable, au bord de l'eau, accentuent le caractère de plage et relaient la ville au second plan.

Plantadas con sauces y arces, las lomas verdes ocupan la mayor parte de la superficie. El paseo de madera y las sombrillas llamativas instaladas en la franja de arena, a orillas del agua, recuerzan su carácter de playa y dejan la ciudad en un segundo plano.

Janet Rosenberg & Associates, Claude Cormier Architectes
Paysagistes, Hariri Pontarini Architects
Toronto, Canada

Rush & Wright Associates, Ashton Raggatt McDougall Architects
Melbourne, Australia

The park provides the services required for the youth population with open recreational spaces. Protection against the wind, already provided by hills, is intensified in the picnic areas, thanks to the inclined metallic shelters.

Het park biedt, met zijn open recreatieruimtes, de door jongeren gewenste diensten. De heuvelruggen van het park bieden op zich al beschutting tegen de wind, hetgeen nog versterkt wordt in de *picknick*-zones dankzij de opstelling van schuine metalen daken.

Der Park dient nicht nur den Kindern und jugendlichen Bewohnern durch seine offen zugänglichen Erholungsbereiche. Der bereits durch die Hügel gegebene Windschutz wird in den Picknickzonen durch schräge Metalldächer verstärkt.

Il parco offre i servizi necessari alla popolazione di giovane età grazie aspazi aperti destinati alla ricreazione. La protezione dal vento, già offerta dal sistema di collinette del parco, è ancora maggiore nelle aree per il picnic, grazie alla collocazione di coperture metalliche inclinate.

Le parc assure aux jeunes son concours en leur proposant des espaces récréatifs ouverts. La protection apportée naturellement contre le vent par les collines du parc est renforcée dans les zones prévues pour pique-niquer grâce à la mise en place de toitures métalliques inclinées.

El parque responde a los requisitos de los jóvenes con espacios recreativos abiertos. La protección contra el viento que ya ofrecen las colinas del parque se refuerza en las zonas destinadas al pícnic, gracias a una serie de cubiertas metálicas inclinadas.

Grupo de Diseño Urbano
Oakland, CA, USA

The park is set down in the middle of a chaotic and dynamically developing urban environment. Various treatments are applied to the flowing stripes that cover the entire park, ranging from solid brick through a more porous surface with brick and grass to stripes that are entirely planted in grass.

Het park ligt midden in een stedelijke ambiance, die zich op chaotische en dynamische wijze ontwikkelt. De stroken die door het park lopen zijn op verschillende manieren ingericht: van solide betegeling tot een meer vochtdoorlatend oppervlak met tegels en gazon en tenslotte stroken die helemaal van gras zijn.

Der Park liegt inmitten einer hektischen und sich dynamisch entwickelnden urbanen Umgebung. Für die fließenden Streifen, die den Boden des gesamten Parks bedecken, wurden verschiedene Materialien verwendet, von massiven Ziegelsteinen über eine eher durchlässige Oberfläche aus Ziegeln und Gras bis hin zu Streifen, die vollständig mit Gras bepflanzt wurden.

Il parco si trova all'interno di un ambiente urbano che si sviluppa in modo caotico e dinamico. Le diverse fasce che attraversano il parco, coprendolo, sono state trattate in modi diversi: dal mattone pieno, a superfici più permeabili con mattoni ed erba fino a fasce interamente a prato.

Le parc se trouve au beau milieu d'un environnement urbain qui se développe de façon chaotique et dynamique. Différents traitements ont été appliqués aux bandes qui parcourent et recouvrent la totalité du parc, des bandes en briques solides à celles recouvertes de gazon, en passant par des surfaces plus flexibles composées à la fois de briques et de pelouse.

El parque está ubicado en medio de un ambiente urbano que se desarrolla de forma caótica y dinámica. Varios tratamientos se han aplicado a las franjas que cubren todo el parque, desde el ladrillo sólido, pasando por una superficie más permeable con ladrillo y césped, hasta llegar a zonas tapizadas por completo de césped.

Urbanus Architecture & Design
Shenzen, China

Ravetllat & Ribas Arquitectes
Barcelona, Spain

The proximity of the sea determined the choice of certain types of vegetation: the flowerbeds are planted with grass and shrubbery in strips parallel to the pathway. The new road layout determines a modification in circulation that directs all traffic towards the road north of the pathway.

De nabijheid van de zee is bepalend geweest voor de keuze voor bijzondere plantensoorten: op de parterres is een gazon aangelegd en zijn er verschillende kruiden geplant in stroken die parallel lopen aan de promenade. Het nieuwe schema leidde tot een wijziging van de verkeerssituatie en het verkeer loopt nu helemaal via de noordelijke rijbaan van de promenade.

Die Auswahl der Pflanzen ist durch die Nähe zum Meer bedingt: Die Geländeoberflächen sind mit Rasen und verschiedenen Gräsern in Reihen parallel zum Weg bepflanzt. Der neue Straßenverlauf hat den Verkehrsfluss verändert und führt ihn vollständig zum nördlichen Rand der Promenade.

L'estrema vicinanza del mare ha condizionato la scelta delle specie vegetali: le aiuole sono coltivate a prato e diversi tipi di erbe a fasce, sorgono parallele al corso. Il nuovo schema stradale modifica la circolazione e la dirige interamente verso la carreggiata nord del corso.

L'extrême proximité de la mer a conditionné le choix de certaines espèces végétales : les parterres sont composés de pelouse et de différentes herbes plantées en bandes parallèles à la promenade. Le nouveau schéma routier a engendré la modification de la circulation et la transfère entièrement vers la chaussée nord de la promenade.

La extrema cercanía del mar ha condicionado la selección de especies vegetales particulares: los parterres están plantados con césped y diferentes hierbas en bandas paralelas al paseo. El nuevo esquema viario provoca la modificación de la circulación y la lleva íntegramente a la calzada norte del paseo.

Janet Rosenberg & Associates
Toronto, Canada

The Bali Memorial is conceived as a meeting point and a place for reflection on the terrorist attacks that occurred on the 12th of October in 2002. Encouraged by authorities, the memorial was built in a location chosen by the victims' families.

De Bali Memorial is bedacht als ontmoetingsruimte en plaats van bezinning over de terroristische aanslagen die op 12 oktober 2002 plaatsvonden. Dit op initiatief van de overheid opgerichte herdenkingsmonument staat op een plaats die is uitgekozen door de familieleden van de slachtoffers.

Bali Memorial ist ein Ort der Begegnung und Reflexion über die auf der Insel verübten Attentate des 12. Oktober 2002. Der Standort für das von offizieller Seite geplante Monument wurde von den Angehörigen der Opfer ausgewählt.

Il Bali Memorial è concepito come luogo d'incontro e di riflessione sugli attacchi terroristi avvenuti nell'isola il 12 ottobre 2002. Promosso dalle autorità, il monumento alla memoria è stato realizzato in un luogo scelto dai famigliari delle vittime.

Le Bali Memorial a été conçu comme un lieu de rencontre et de réflexion sur les attaques terroristes qui se sont produites sur l'île le 12 octobre 2002. Avec le soutien des autorités, le monument commémoratif a été érigé à un endroit choisi par les parents des victimes.

El Bali Memorial está concebido como un lugar de encuentro y de reflexión dedicado a los ataques terroristas ocurridos en la isla el 12 octubre de 2002. Impulsado por las autoridades, el monumento se ha realizado en un lugar escogido por los familiares de las víctimas.

Janet Rosenberg & Associates
Ottawa, Canada

Donaldson & Warm Architects
Perth, Australia
(opposite page)

Agence APS Paysagistes DPLG Associés
Valencia, Spain

Landslag ehf Landslagsarkitektar FÍLA
Reykjavík, Iceland
(opposite page)

Taylor Cullity Lethlean
Melbourne, Australia
(left)

David Irwin/Isthmus Group
Manukau, New Zealand
(opposite page, left)

Taylor Cullity Lethlean
Melbourne, Australia
(opposite page, top right)

Rosa Grena Kliass Arquitetura Paisagística
São Paulo, Brasil
(opposite page, bottom right)

Taylor Cullity Lethlean
Melbourne, Australia

NIP Paysage
Montreal, Canada

Verzone Woods Architectes
Latas, Spain

446

A rich and contrasting variety of materials and pavements intersect. As viewed from above in plan, they have a painterly effect. From the ground level viewpoint of a stroller, the crisp details offer a constantly changing visual interest, set off by the backdrop of dark green rolling foothills beyond.

Een rijke en contrasterende verscheidenheid aan materialen en plaveisel snijdt elkaar. Van bovenaf gezien, als kaart, heeft het een pittoresk effect. Gezien vanaf de grond, als een voorbijganger, hebben de frisse details een visueel belang dat voortdurend verandert en contrasteert met de groene omgeving van de nabijgelegen heuvels.

In Las Margas trifft eine weit gefächerte und kontrastreiche Bandbreite von Materialien aufeinander. Von oben gesehen erzielen sie eine malerische Wirkung. Aus der Perspektive eines Spaziergängers zu ebener Erde bieten die klaren Details abwechslungsreiche visuelle Eindrücke, die sich deutlich vor dem dunkelgrünen Hintergrund der bewegten Bergkette abzeichnen.

Elemento fondamentale è la commistione di una ricca e contrastante varietà di materiali. Visto dall'alto, l'effetto è decisamente pittorico. Dal livello del suolo, così come appare ai passanti, l'attenzione è catturata dai dettagli che cambiano costantemente e contrastano con la tonalità verde scuro delle colline vicine.

Des matériaux et des revêtements, variés et contrastés, s'entrecroisent. Vu d'en haut, l'effet est pictural. Vu depuis le sol, à travers les yeux d'un passant, les détails ont un intérêt visuel qui change constamment et tranche avec le vert foncé des collines voisines.

Una rica y contrastante variedad de materiales y pavimentos se entrecruzan. Visto desde arriba, el efecto es decidamente pictórico. Desde el nivel del suelo, desde el punto de vista de un caminante, los detalles tienen un interés visual que cambia constantemente y contrastan con el entorno verde oscuro de las colinas cercanas.

NIP Paysage
Ottawa, Canada

Claudi Aguiló/Data AE Arquitectura i Enginyeria
Sant Cristòfol, Spain
(opposite page)

John Cunningham Architects, Landworks Studio, Office DA
Boston, MA, USA
(left)

Burger Landschaftsarchitekten
Unterföhring, Germany
(right)

John Cunningham Architects, Landworks Studio, Office DA
Boston, MA, USA
(opposite page)

Fragmented shards of alternating ipe wood and aluminum panels form the thin deck surface that floats above the undulating ground surface. Plantings are placed to block direct views into private ground level windows. Not yet installed are the fiber optic light lines and stainless steel cable canopy.

Het smalle oppervlak van het dak dat boven de golvende vloer zweeft, is gevormd door elkaar afwisselende fragmenten van ipé-hout en aluminium panelen. Er zijn boompjes geplant tegen inkijk via de ramen van de benedenverdieping. In deze afbeelding zijn de glasvezellijnen en de baldakijn van roestvrij stalen kabels nog niet te zien.

Sich abwechselnde Flächen von Magnolienholz- und Aluminiumpaneelen bilden ein dünnes Deck, das über die sich wellende Bodenoberfläche treibt. Pflanzen verhindern den direkten Einblick in die privaten Räume im Erdgeschoss. In diesem Bild noch nicht installiert sind die Glasfaserkabel sowie der Baldachin aus Edelstahlseilen.

La delicata superficie di copertura che fluttua sopra al suolo ondulante è formata da frammenti alternati di legno di Ipè e pannelli di alluminio. Sono state messe a dimora diverse piante per impedire la visuale diretta verso le finestre del piano terra. In questa immagine non sono ancora state installate le linee di fibra ottica e la copertura di cavi di acciaio inossidabile.

La mince toiture qui flotte au-dessus du sol ondulant est composée de fragments alternatifs de bois d'Ipé et de panneaux d'aluminium. Des plantes ont été semées pour bloquer la vue directe vers l'intérieur à travers les fenêtres de l'étage inférieur. Sur cette image, les lignes de fibre optique et les câbles en acier inoxydable n'ont pas encore été installés.

La delgada superficie de cubierta que flota sobre el suelo ondulante está formada por fragmentos alternativos de madera de Ipé y paneles de aluminio. Se han sembrado plantas para bloquear la vista directa al interior de las ventanas de la planta baja. En esta imagen aún no se han instalado las líneas de fibra óptica y el dosel de cables de acero inoxidable.

SLA
Copenhagen, Denmark

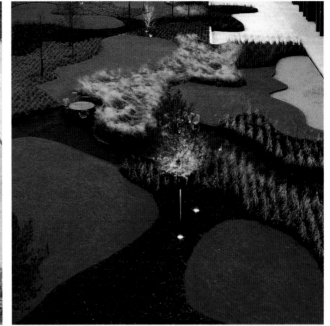

Aspect Studios
Bondi, Australia

Loosely parallel strips constructed in concrete contain a palette of native materials. The water course is underlain with rounded local rocks. White gravel contrasts with the plantings. The plants are all species indigenous to the nearby Australian coast. The effect is equally impressive whether viewed from above in plan, or at ground level.

De stroken die vagelijk parallel in cement zijn aangelegd hebben het kleurenpalet van inheemse materialen. Het water stroomt door een kanaal over een bed van plaatselijke stenen. Witte kiezels contrasteren met de tuinen. De planten zijn inheemse soorten van de nabijgelegen Australische kust. Het effect is hetzelfde, zowel van boven af gezien als vanaf de grond.

Die Beete, die durch fast parallel laufende Betonbänder strukturiert sind, beherbergen verschiedene einheimische Pflanzen, die typisch für die australische Küste sind, mit Gestein und Kies im Wechsel. Im Wasserbecken liegen Steine aus der Gegend. Der Garten beeindruckt mit seinem linearen Aufbau nicht nur zu ebener Erde, sondern auch aus der Vogelperspektive.

Fasce vagamente parallele costruite in cemento comprendono una varietà di materiali originari del luogo. Dentro al canale, l'acqua scorre su un letto di pietre locali. La ghiaia bianca crea un contrasto con i giardini. Le piante sono specie indigene della vicina costa australiana. La vista dall'alto o dal livello del terreno produce lo stesso effetto.

Des bandes vaguement parallèles construites en ciment revêtent toute une palette de matériaux locaux. L'eau coule dans le canal sur un lit de pierres locales. Les gravillons blancs contrastent avec les jardins. Les plantes sont des espèces originaires de la côte australienne voisine. L'effet produit est identique, qu'il soit perçu depuis le haut ou bien depuis le sol.

Franjas vagamente paralelas construidas con cemento contienen una paleta de materiales nativos. El agua corre en el canal sobre un lecho de piedras locales. La gravilla blanca contrasta con los jardines. Las plantas son especies procedentes de la cercana costa australiana. El efecto es el mismo, tanto si se observa desde arriba como desde el suelo.

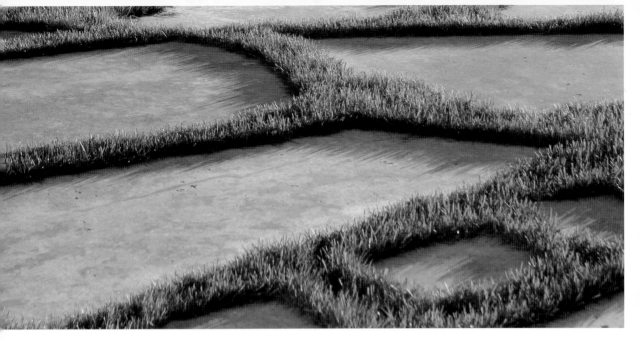

Burger Landschaftsarchitekten
Unterföhring, Germany

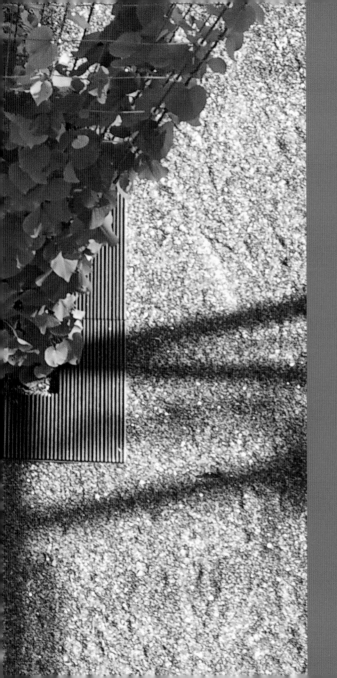

Urban furniture

Stadtmöblierung

Mobilier urbain

Straatmeubilair

Arredi urbani

Mobiliario urbano

The elements and furniture that make up the urban space, referred to as equipment or furniture, are all objects that are used and integrated into the urban environment. These should be functional, aesthetic, and harmonic and provide specific benefits for the citizens. During the last decade, in large cities major advertising campaigns have been developed integrated into urban elements such as lights, illuminated posts, telephone booths, etc. Urban planning is no necessary with the rise of megalopolises and specialists attempt to reverse existing urban decay and try to implement changes to improve the urban quality of life of its inhabitants. In this sense, the order of the elements that make up the urban space can be achieved with proper design, giving the city an identity that distinguishes it from others. Street furniture identifies and gives cities personality. When designing street furniture, features that should be considered include: weather-resistance and the aggressiveness of the urban environment, the wear and tear over time while in use and ease of upkeep and maintenance to achieve an efficient urban space.

If the furniture is not suitable, maintenance costs will be too high and the poor manufacturing will involve a risk in the quality of the urban structure. Avoid ephemeral and poor quality designs opt for harmonic and functional items that integrate into the landscape. In this sense, advanced technologies and quality materials are favored that create excellent furniture designed to improve the quality of life for those who enjoy it.

Sont appelés équipement ou mobilier urbain tous les éléments, meubles et objets utilisés et intégrés à l'environnement urbain. Ceux-ci doivent être fonctionnels, esthétiques, harmonieux et apporter les bénéfices particuliers dont ont besoin les citoyens. Au cours de la dernière décennie, les grandes villes ont mis en place des campagnes publicitaires intégrées à des éléments urbains tels que les feux, les poteaux d'éclairage, les cabines téléphoniques, etc. La planification urbaine est devenue nécessaire avec l'essor des mégapoles ; les spécialistes tentent de réparer la détérioration urbaine et de mettre en place des changements visant à améliorer la qualité de vie urbaine des habitants. En ce sens, l'ordre des éléments composant l'espace urbain peut s'exprimer au travers d'un design approprié, dotant les villes d'une identité personnelle. Dans la conception du mobilier urbain, il faut tenir compte de la résistance aux effets climatiques et à l'hostilité de l'environnement, de sa détérioration au fil de son utilisation, ainsi que de ses conditions de conservation et d'entretien, afin d'obtenir un espace urbain efficace. Si le mobilier urbain n'est pas approprié, les frais d'entretien seront excessifs et la fabrication précaire entraînera un risque quant à la qualité de la structure urbaine. Il convient d'éviter les designs éphémères et de basse qualité, et de miser davantage sur des éléments harmonieux et fonctionnels, qui s'intègrent au paysage. En ce sens, la tendance actuelle est de compter sur les technologies avancées et les matériaux de qualité, ce qui permet de concevoir un mobilier de qualité visant à améliorer le bien-être de ceux qui en profiteront.

Elemente und Möbel des städtischen Raums, so genannte Stadtmöbel oder Straßenmöbel, sind in die Stadtlandschaft integrierte Gebrauchsgegenstände. Sie müssen funktionell, ästhetisch und harmonisch sein und den Bürgern ihre spezifischen Vorteile bieten. Im letzten Jahrzehnt wurden in den Großstädten große Werbekampagnen durchgeführt, in die städtische Elemente wie Ampeln, Straßenlaternen, Telefonzellen usw. einbezogen wurden. Mit dem Boom der Megastädte wurde die Stadtplanung notwendig und die Spezialisten versuchen, den Verfall der Städte umzukehren und Veränderungen zur Verbesserung der Qualität der Städte und der Lebensqualität ihrer Bewohner einzuführen. In diesem Sinn kann man durch ein entsprechendes Design die Ordnung der Elemente, aus denen der städtische Raum besteht, bestimmen und den Städten eine eigene Identität verleihen, die sie von anderen unterscheidet. Die Straßenmöblierung verleiht den Städten Identität und Persönlichkeit. Beim Design dieser Straßenmöbel müssen die Widerstandsfähigkeit gegenüber Wettereinflüssen und der Aggressivität des städtischen Umfelds berücksichtigt werden, die Abnutzung, die sie während ihres Gebrauchs unterliegen, sowie eine Pflegeleichtigkeit und einfache Wartung, um eine wirkungsvolle städtische Umwelt zu erzielen. Wenn die Straßenmöbel ungeeignet sind, schießen die Ausgaben für deren Wartung in die Höhe, die nachlässige Herstellung führt zu Risiken in Bezug auf die Qualität der städtischen Struktur. Kurzlebige Designs und Ausführungen von minderer Qualität müssen vermieden werden und man sollte auf Elemente setzen, die sich harmonisch und funktionell in die Stadtlandschaft einfügen. In diesem Sinn setzt man heute fortschrittliche Technologien und hochwertige Materialien ein, die es erlauben, Qualitätsmobiliar zu entwerfen und so die Lebensqualität derer, die es benutzen, zu verbessern.

De elementen en meubels die in de stedelijke ruimte staan en die voorzieningen of straatmeubilair worden genoemd, zijn alle voorwerpen die in de stedelijke omgeving worden gebruikt en daarbinnen zijn geïntegreerd. Ze moeten functioneel, esthetisch en harmonieus zijn en tegemoetkomen aan de behoeften van de inwoners. Gedurende het afgelopen decennium zijn er in de grote steden reclamecampagnes geïntegreerd in stedelijke elementen zoals stoplichten, verlichte zuilen, telefooncellen, etc. De opkomst van metropolen heeft stedelijke ordening nodig gemaakt en deskundigen proberen de teloorgang een halt toe te roepen en wijzigingen door te voeren om de levenskwaliteit van de inwoners te verbeteren. In die zin kan de ordening van de elementen waaruit de stedelijke ruimte bestaat worden bereikt door een geschikt ontwerp en door de steden een identiteit te geven waardoor zij zich onderscheiden van de rest. De stedelijke voorzieningen voorzien steden van een eigen identiteit en meer persoonlijkheid. In dit ontwerp van straatmeubilair moet worden gekeken naar de resistentheid tegen weersinvloeden en naar de agressiviteit van de stedelijke omgeving, de mate waarin ze door de tijd worden aangetast en naar mogelijkheden voor bewaring en behoud. Dit alles om een efficiënte stedelijke ruimte te krijgen. Als het straatmeubilair niet geschikt is, zullen de onderhoudskosten teveel oplopen en een gebrekkige fabricage brengt een risico voor de kwaliteit van de stedelijke structuur met zich mee. Kortstondige en kwaliteitsarme ontwerpen moeten voorkomen en er moet worden ingezet op harmonieuze en functionele elementen die in het landschap integreren. In dat opzicht wordt tegenwoordig gekozen voor geavanceerde technieken en materialen van kwaliteit die de levenskwaliteit van de stedelingen te verbeteren.

Gli elementi e gli arredi presenti nello spazio urbano, denominati attrezzature o arredi urbani, sono tutti quegli oggetti che si utilizzano e fanno parte dell'ambiente urbano. Si tratta di elementi che devono essere necessariamente funzionali, estetici, armonici e offrire benefici specifici ai cittadini. Durante quest'ultimo decennio nelle grandi città sono state lanciate grandi campagne pubblicitarie che hanno sfruttato elementi urbani quali semafori, lampioni illuminati, cabine telefoniche, ecc. La pianificazione urbana è diventata necessaria con l'estensione delle megalopoli e gli specialisti cercano di invertire l'esistente deterioramento urbano cercando di implementare soluzioni per migliorare la qualità della vita urbana dei suoi abitanti. In questo senso, l'ordine degli elementi che compongono lo spazio urbano è possibile grazie a progetti adeguati che siano in grado di dare alle città un'identità che le distingua dalle altre. L'arredo urbano identifica e conferisce personalità alle città. Nel progettare l'arredo urbano, naturalmente, non bisogna trascurare la resistenza agli effetti climatici ed all'aggressività dell'ambiente urbano, il deterioramento legato al trascorrere del tempo durante la loro vita utile, la facilità di conservazione e la manutenzione per ottenere uno spazio urbano efficiente.
Se l'arredo urbano non è quello adeguato, i costi di manutenzione saranno eccessivi e la precaria fabbricazione comporterà un rischio che inciderà negativamente sulla qualità dell'arredo urbano. È necessario evitare i design effimeri e di poca qualità e puntare su elementi facilmente integrabili nel paesaggio, armonici e funzionali. In questo senso, oggi giorno si punta su tecnologie avanzate e su materiali di qualità che consentono di progettare arredi di qualità migliorando la qualità di vita di coloro che ne fanno uso.

Los elementos y los muebles que componen el espacio urbano, conocidos como equipamiento o mobiliario urbano, son todos aquellos objetos que se utilizan y se integran en el entorno urbano. Deben ser funcionales, estéticos, armónicos y proporcionar beneficios específicos a sus ciudadanos. Durante la última década, en las grandes ciudades se han desarrollado campañas publicitarias integradas en elementos urbanos como semáforos, postes iluminados, cabinas telefónicas, etc. La planificación urbana se ha hecho necesaria con el auge de las megalópolis y los especialistas intentan revertir el deterioro urbano existente e implantar cambios de mejora de la calidad de vida urbana de sus habitantes. Es en este sentido, el orden de los elementos que componen el espacio urbano se puede conseguir con un diseño adecuado, dotando a la ciudad de una identidad que la distinga de las demás. El equipamiento urbano identifica y da personalidad a las ciudades. En el diseño del mobiliario urbano hay que tener en cuenta la resistencia a los efectos climáticos y la agresividad del entorno urbano, el deterioro que sufre durante el tiempo que permanece en uso y la facilidad de conservación y mantenimiento para conseguir un espacio urbano eficiente.
Si el mobiliario urbano no es adecuado, serán excesivos los costes de mantenimiento y la precaria fabricación conllevará un riesgo de la calidad de la estructura urbana. Hay que evitar los diseños efímeros y de poca calidad y apostar por elementos que se integren con el paisaje, armónicos y funcionales. Por ello, actualmente se opta por tecnologías avanzadas y materiales de calidad que permiten diseñar mobiliario de calidad que mejora la vida de aquellos que lo disfrutan.

Burger Landschaftsarchitekten
Munich, Germany

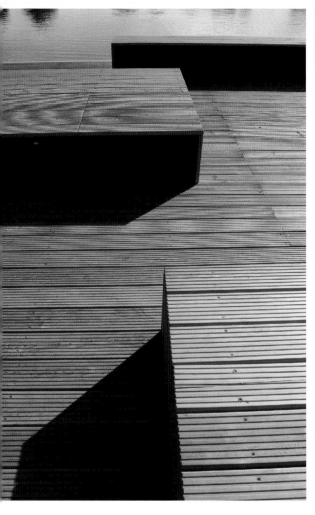

Hutterreimann & Cejka Landschaftsarchitekten
Wernigerode, Germany

AllesWirdGut Architektur
Innichen, Italy

Carlos Martínez Architekten, Pipilotti Rist/Hauser & Wirth
St. Gallen, Switzerland
(opposite page)

The urban fixture elements seem to emerge from the ground and their soft and rounded shapes contrast with the marked lines of the surrounding buildings. The placement of these elements, accompanied by the intensity of the lights, creates a meditative and comfortable atmosphere in apparently adverse surroundings.

De elementen van stadsmeubilair lijken uit de grond op te duiken en de zachte en ronde silhouetten contrasteren met de strakke lijnen van de omringende gebouwen. Deze opstelling van de elementen waaruit het meubilair bestaat, vergezeld door de intense verlichting, scheppen een sfeer van gezelligheid en comfort in een schijnbaar ongunstige omgeving.

Das Mobiliar scheint aus dem Boden zu wachsen und kontrastiert durch seine sanften, abgerundeten Formen mit den harten Konturen der umliegenden Gebäude. Durch die spezielle Beleuchtung wird inmitten der kalten Umgebung eine gemütliche Atmosphäre geschaffen.

Gli elementi dell'arredo urbano sembrano emergere dal suolo e il loro profilo, delicato e arrotondato, contrasta con le linee nette degli edifici circostanti. Questa disposizione degli elementi che costituiscono l'arredo, sommata all'intensità delle luci, crea un'atmosfera di raccoglimento e comodità in un ambiente apparentemente ostile.

Les éléments du mobilier urbain semblent émerger du sol, leurs formes douces et arrondies contrastent avec les lignes marquées des édifices environnants. Cet agencement des éléments qui composent le mobilier, associé à l'intensité des lumières, créent une atmosphère propice au recueillement et au confort, dans un environnement d'apparence hostile.

Los elementos del mobiliario urbano parecen emerger del suelo y sus siluetas suaves y redondeadas contrastan con las marcadas líneas de los edificios circundantes. Esta disposición de los elementos que componen el mobiliario, junto con la intensidad de las luces, crean una atmósfera de recogimiento y comodidad en un entorno aparentemente adverso.

Donaldson & Warm Architects
Perth, Australia

De Amicis Architetti
Settimo Milanese, Italy
(opposite page)

David Irwin/Isthmus Group
Manukau, New Zealand
(left)

Topotek 1
(right)

David Irwin/Isthmus Group
Manukau, New Zealand
(opposite page)

Ravetllat & Ribas Arquitectes
Barcelona, Spain

NIP Paysage
Montreal, Canada
(opposite page)

Groupings of bright green seating pods are housed in super-minimalist gazebos. A simple three-part palette of wood (the predominant material), gravel and spare greenery define this composition of subtle cants and syncopated rhythms.

Samenstellingen van groene zitplaatsen zijn geconcentreerd in deze super-minimalistische priëlen. Een simpel houten platform (hoofdmateriaal), bestaande uit drie delen, het grind en de her en der verspreide groenzones definiëren de compositie van vlakken met subtiele hellingen en syncopische ritmes.

Sitzgruppen aus leuchtend grünem Kunststoff werden von äußerst minimalistischen Pavillons „beherbergt". Schlichte Materialien wie Holz und Kies und eine zurückhaltende Bepflanzung strukturieren den Raum.

Sotto questi pergolati minimalisti si trova una concentrazione di sedili verdi. Una semplice piattaforma in legno di tre parti (materiale principale), la ghiaia e gli occasionali spazi verdi definiscono la composizione dei piani, leggermente inclinati e marcati da ritmi sincopati.

Des ensembles de sièges verts sont regroupés sous ces tonnelles extrêmement minimalistes. Une simple plate-forme en bois en trois parties (matériau principal), les gravillons et les espaces verts occasionnels définissent la composition de plans subtilement inclinés et de rythmes syncopés.

Bajo unas glorietas extremadamente minimalistas se han dispuesto unos conjuntos de asientos verdes. Una simple plataforma de madera de tres partes (el material principal), la gravilla y los ocasionales espacios verdes definen la composición de planos sutilmente inclinados y de ritmos sincopados.

Despang Architekten
Hannover, Germany

The rust-colored corten steel containers contrast nicely with the simple gray gravel covering the courtyard.

Die rostfarbenen Container aus Corten-Stahl heben sich hübsch von dem einfachen grauen Kies ab, der den Hof bedeckt.

Les conteneurs en acier Corten de couleur rouille forment un contraste agréable avec la simplicité des graviers gris qui recouvrent la cour intérieure.

De roestkleurige cortenstalen bakken contrasteren mooi met de eenvoudige grijze kiezellaag op de binnenplaats.

I colorati contenitori in acciaio ossidato creano un piacevole contrastano con la semplice ghiaia grigia che ricopre il cortile.

Los contenedores de acero corten rojizo crean un agradable contraste con la gravilla gris que cubre el patio.

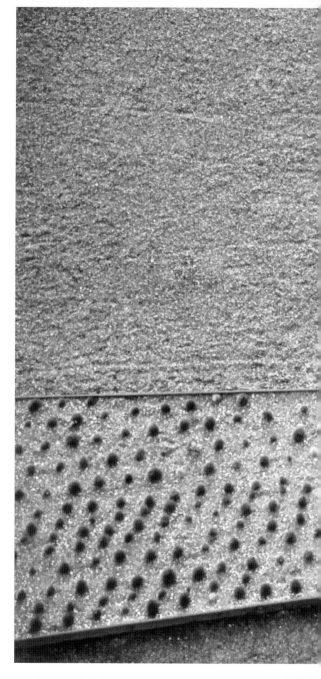

Delta Vorm Groep
Utrecht, The Netherlands

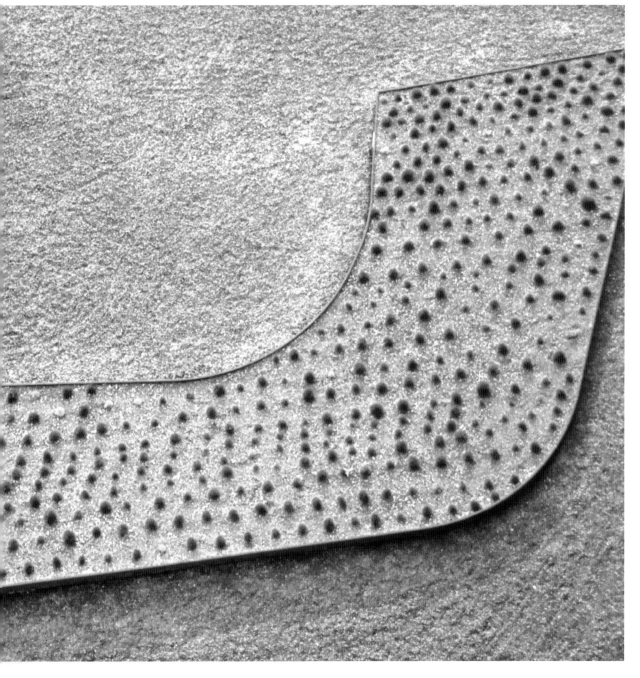

The light installation had to be waterproof, low power, low maintenance, fully automatic, and create dynamic shows. Londoners crossing the square to reach nearby Liverpool Street station can now find their way around more easily.

De lichtinstallatie moest waterproof, energiebesparend, onderhoudsvriendelijk, en volautomatisch zijn en dynamische shows creëren. De inwoners van Londen die het plein oversteken naar het Liverpool Street station kunnen nu gemakkelijker de weg vinden.

Die Beleuchtung muss wasserdicht sein, einen niedrigen Energiebedarf haben, pflegeleicht und vollautomatisch sein und eine gute Sicht ermöglichen. Londoner, die den Platz überqueren, um zu der nahegelegenen Liverpool Street Station zu gelangen, haben es jetzt leichter, den Weg zu finden.

L'installazione leggera doveva essere idrofuga, a bassa potenza, minima manutenzione, totalmente automatizzata e generare dinamismo. I londinesi che attraversano la piazza diretti alla vicina Liverpool Street station trovano la strada più facilmente.

L'éclairage devait être waterproof et à basse tension, mais il devait également demander peu d'entretien, être entièrement automatique et créer des affichages dynamiques. Les Londoniens qui traversent le parc pour rejoindre Liverpool Street peuvent désormais se repérer plus facilement.

Las luces tenían que ser impermeables, de poca potencia, bajo mantenimiento, totalmente automáticas y crear un efecto dinámico. Los londinenses que ahora cruzan la plaza en dirección a la estación de Liverpool Street podrán encontrar más fácilmente el camino.

Maurice Brill Lighting Design
London, UK

Stanton Williams
London, UK

3LHD
Rijeka, Croatia

Ábalos & Herreros, Escofet
Barcelona, Spain
(this page)

The designers took their inspiration for this pink serpent-shaped resting space from the human spinal column.

De menselijke ruggengraat vormde de bron van inspiratie voor de ontwerpers van deze roze slangvormige ontspanningsruimte.

Die Designer wurden für diesen rosafarbenen schlangenförmigen Ruheplatz von der menschlichen Wirbelsäule inspiriert.

La colonna vertebrale umana è stata fonte d'ispirazione per i progettisti di questo spazio di riposo, rosa dalla forma serpeggiante.

Pour cet espace de détente rose en forme de serpent, les designers se sont inspirés de la colonne vertébrale humaine.

Los diseñadores se inspiraron en la columna vertebral humana para crear esta serpenteante zona de descanso de color rosa.

Gonzalez Haase / AAS
Bremen, Germany

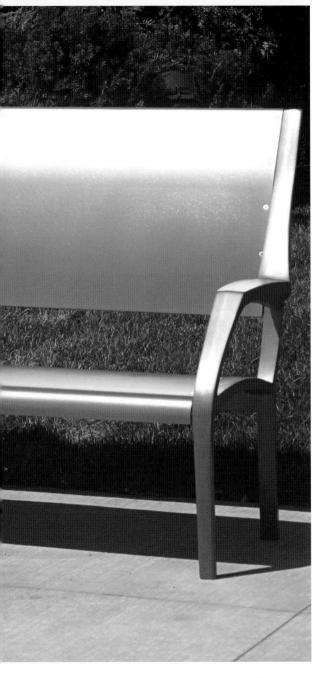

The bench's profile integrates anthropomorphic forms with comfortable powdercoat-colored material and finishes.

Die Form der Bank verbindet anthropomorphe Formen mit einem angenehmen pulverbeschichteten Material und Oberflächen.

La silhouette du banc associe des formes anthropomorphes à des matériaux et finitions recouverts de peintures en poudre appliquéees par projection électrostatique.

Het profiel van de bank combineert menselijke vormen met comfortabele, door middel van poederlak gekleurde materialen.

La sagoma della panchina unisce la forma antropomorfa al comfort del materiale e delle rifiniture color polvere

El perfil del banco aúna formas antropomórficas y cómodos materiales acabados en pintura electrostática.

Gustafson Guthrie Nichol
Chicago, IL, USA

Furnishings blend into the textilelike surface: concrete elements serve as seating and parking-space barriers. Dark and light bands define the open space while Japanese cherry trees subtly line the avenue.

Het meubilair wordt gecombineerd met een textielachtige oppervlak: betonnen elementen doen dienst als zitting e barrières voor parkeerplaatsen. Donkere en lichte stroken definiëren de open ruimte, terwijl Japanse kersen de laan op subtiele wijze belijnen.

Die Möblierung verbindet sich mit der gewebeähnlichen Oberfläche: Elemente aus Beton dienen als Sitze und Parkplatz-Begrenzungen. Dunkle und helle Bänder umgrenzen den offenen Platz und entlang der Straße bilden Japanische Kirschbäume ein elegantes Spalier.

La mobilia s'integra in una superficie che sembra tessuto: gli elementi in calcestruzzo fungono da sedili separando i posti macchina. Strisce scure e chiare delimitano lo spazio aperto mentre dei ciliegi giapponesi solcano sottilmente il viale.

Les équipements mobiliers se mêlent aux surfaces d'apparence textile : des éléments en béton forment des sièges et des barrières entre les places de stationnement. Des bandes claires et foncées délimitent l'espace ouvert alors que les cerisiers japonais bordent subtilement l'avenue.

El mobiliario combina bien con la superficie tipo textil: los elementos de hormigón sirven de asiento y de separadores. Las bandas claras y oscuras definen el espacio abierto, y los cerezos japoneses envuelven delicadamente la avenida.

Topotek 1
Dreiech, Germany

Wraignt & Associates
Wellington, New Zealand

(Parenthesis) questions the individual's relationship with public spaces: to walk through it or around it? The corner of Mont-Royal Avenue and St. Hubert Street is a busy and wider-than-usual intersection.

(Parentheses) stellen de relatie tussen het individu en openbare ruimtes aan de orde: er doorheen lopen of rondlopen? De hoek van de Mont-Royal Avenue en St. Hubert Street is een drukke kruising die breder is dan gebruikelijk.

(Einschub) hinterfragt das Verhältnis des Einzelnen zu öffentlichen Plätzen: durchlaufen oder außen herumgehen? Die Ecke Mont-Royal Avenue und St. Hubert Street ist eine belebte Kreuzung und größer als üblich.

(Parentesi) Ci si interroga sui rapporti tra l'individuo e lo spazio pubblico: attraversarlo o girarci intorno? L'angolo tra la Mont-Royal Avenue e St. Hubert Street è un incrocio affollato einsolitamente ampio.

(Parenthèse) remet en question le rapport de l'individu aux espaces publics : s'agit-il de les traverser ou de les contourner ? L'angle de Mont-Royal Avenue et de St. Hubert Street est une intersection très fréquentée et plus étendue que la normale.

(Parenthesis) indaga en la relación entre el individuo y los espacios públicos: ¿rodearlos o cruzarlos? La intersección entre Mont-Royal Avenue y la St. Hubert Street es un espacio ajetreado y más ancho de lo normal.

Justin Dubé-Fahmy & Hubert Pelletier
Montreal, Canada

Agence Concepto
Rouen, France

A lighting scenography was created to link this space to the right riverbank and to the city center.

Een lichtscenografie is gecreëerd om deze ruimte te verbinden met de rechter rivieroever en met de binnenstad.

Um diesen Bereich mit dem rechten Flussufer und dem Stadtzentrum zu verbinden, wurde eine Licht-Szenerie gestaltet.

È stata creata una scenografia luminosa per collegare questo spazio alla sponda destra e al centro città.

Une scénographie lumineuse a été créée pour relier cet espace à la rive droite et au centre-ville.

Se ha creado una escenografía luminosa para conectar este espacio con la ribera derecha del río y el centro de la ciudad.